THE TACKLE BOX

By Vince Daubenspeck

Exploring the lures that attract,
hook and destroy men

INTRODUCTION

AM AN AVID fish enthusiast and fisherman. Put me anywhere near a body of water, and I will be in it, or on it, and either netting, hooking, trapping or spearing the fish that live there. I will, subsequently, put them in an aquarium for observation or in a cooler for later consumption. I cannot remember a time in my life when the water and all the creatures in it did not mesmerize me. As a child, I truly could empathize with Don Knotts in *The Incredible Mr. Limpet* when he looked down into the water and said, "I wish I were a fish."

For me, bodies of water serve as giant erasers. They have the magical ability to erase the trials, tribulations and cares of the world, even if only temporarily. When I am on the shore, casting a lure, or lying on the seabed, waiting for a fish to swim in to the range of my speargun, all of those other things in life don't even exist. And I know, for most men, water has a lot of the same qualities. If it were not so, Bass Pro Shops would not have done $3.83Billion in business with 18,000 employees in roughly 50 stores in 2011. A man can literally walk into an Outdoor World showroom and take a mini-vacation on the spot.

I recently had the pleasure of visiting a store in Ft Myers, Florida and took a mini-vacation while I was attending my oldest son's wedding. As I was driving on the highway, I could see the big bass sign on the front of the store and I could feel the black hole super gravity pulling me there. Just like encountering the Borg, resistance was futile, and luckily it was not the same day as the wedding. Once I walked in, the eye-candy was overwhelming. There were all kinds of trophy fish on the walls, rows of rods, lanes of lures, a gallery of guns and ammo, a parking lot of boats and a two-story aquarium with game fish. And that was merely a part of the bottom floor.

I am mostly drawn to the fishing lure sections of sports stores. Some of my favorite times with my dad were camping and fishing trips to Lake Patagonia in southern Arizona and the lure sections always remind me of those trips. They also remind me of the mustard colored tackle box with my dad's arsenal of weapons. Jitterbugs, Big O's, Rapalas, Poppers, and Bombers are just the tip of the iceberg of fishing memory catalysts for me.

Above: My Dad showing off his trophy bass at Lake Patagonia.

Facing Page: My Dad fly-fishing an Oregon river.

I HAVE COME THAT THEY MIGHT HAVE LIFE AND THAT THEY MIGHT HAVE IT MORE ABUNDANTLY. John 10:10b

When I analyze my desire to collect fishing lures, it reminds me of the weapons the enemy has at his disposal to catch me. One thing that upsets me is how easily I can fall to certain sins in my life. As I was discussing this the other day with my wife, I told her that we had a great future ahead of us. I told her we both should be aware of our individual and unique weaknesses and pitfalls. That great work in our future could be at risk, especially if we do not recognize the cracks in our armor and address those problems. I further relayed how I was looking at our weaknesses through a military lens (being a retired military aviator) and was thinking about writing a book about men and their weaknesses from a military vantage point. I went on to say that we could also look at men's weaknesses from the viewpoint of sports metaphors. But, in my opinion, there is nothing closer to the real life of men and their penchant for sin than the analogy of a crafty, wise Fisherman in pursuit of his game. He wants to catch me and he knows my personality. He knows what lures work for me, and he is very successful at filling his cooler with my friends, the husbands of my friends, and if we are not vigilant, you and me.

This book attempts to put into plain, understandable, and actionable language how we, specifically men, need to be aware of the environment we live in and how dangerous it can be to our families and our spiritual lives. After we are aware of our environment and our own personalities, we need to know how to protect ourselves from the Fisherman and his lures. In section III, I put forward clear and practical strategies to prevent us from falling prey to the lures that are specifically designed to get each and every one of us to bite. Finally, in Section IV, I talk about what to do when we discover that we are hooked. I hope that through this examination, we can all become more cognizant of the Fisherman and his incessant desire for our failure. Instead, let's look to our Lord and Savior for guidance and strength, as He only wants our ultimate success.

ACKNOWLEDGEMENTS

IN JUNE OF 2012, I had a Pulmonary Embolism and, according to my gifted ER doctors, almost died. God mercifully and purposefully shut off all real estate work for me and I sat in the back yard and stared at the ocean for months. I wondered. I prayed. I read. And I questioned many things. My wife did not quite know what to do with me, but that was fine as I did not quite know what to do with me either. During that time, I leaned very heavily on the Word and I read and reread A. W. Tozier's *The Pursuit of God* several times, among other writings. Within a very short period of time, I started to wake up with things on my mind that I needed to write down. The first story that consumed me was a little novel called *Crown of Thorns* that was published a few months later. Once that was finished, I started waking up with a men's ministry book on my mind, which you are now holding in your hands. I questioned what was happening with and to me all along the way, but without the help and encouragement of several people, it would not have come to fruition.

First and foremost, to the creator of purpose and the giver of life, thank you for stopping me in my tracks and giving me dreams. I pray that I seized the moment and got it right. Thank you for putting people in my life that pushed, pulled, encouraged and even gave me guilt trips along the way.

Thank you to my beautiful, spirit-filled wife who prayed without ceasing and took care of me along the journey. Hopefully, she does not have to stick needles in me ever again.

Thank you to Mark and Diane Button for being such great friends, neighbors and editors extraordinaire. It is truly a blessing to entwine our families and lives with yours.

Thank you Ben and Christy Pierce. This would not have been anything beyond an exercise in creative writing without your constant encouragement and vision for what you believed this would become. It was such a joy to have met you in the spring of 2009 and see how close we have become, even though we live so far apart.

Above: Mykal, Jacqui, and Carter on the day I caught my first Marlin.

Facing Page: Newly married James Bradshaw and my daughter Jacqui giving a little tribute to her spearfishing crazy Dad.

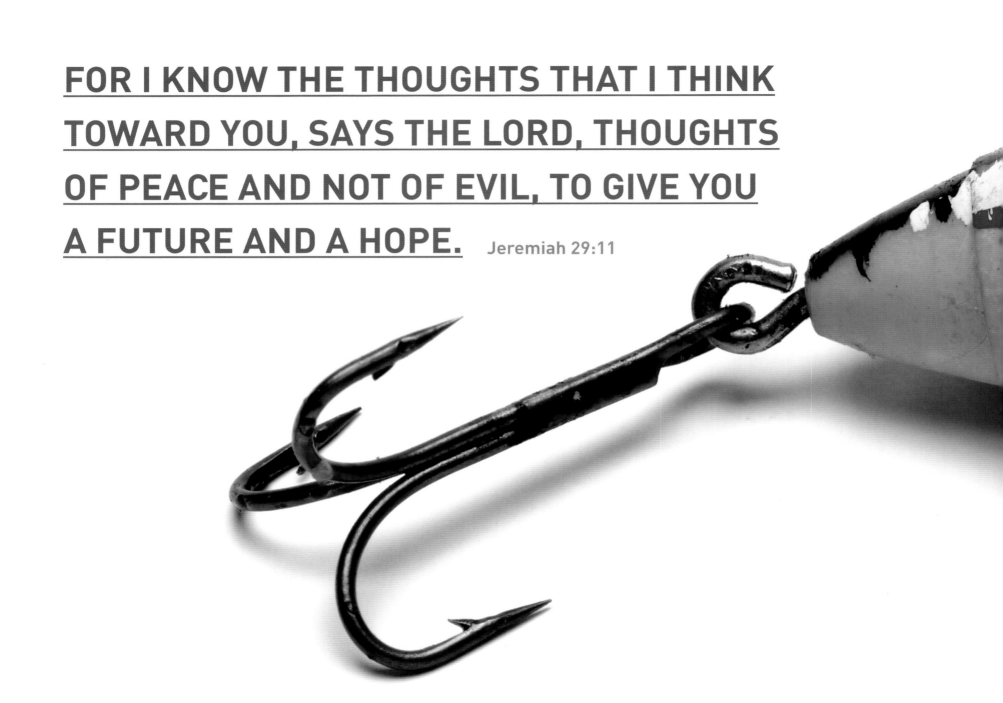

FOR I KNOW THE THOUGHTS THAT I THINK TOWARD YOU, SAYS THE LORD, THOUGHTS OF PEACE AND NOT OF EVIL, TO GIVE YOU A FUTURE AND A HOPE. Jeremiah 29:11

What is your fish personality type?

STYLES OF FISHING

BEFORE WE DIVE IN (I love all the metaphors available!) to the discussion of fish, to the discussion of fish, I think it would be helpful to take some time and talk a little about the types of fishing that people employ. Most of you are familiar with some of the many ways to catch fish. You can picture the mighty angler, strapped into the deck chair of the charter boat, giant rod bending, as they try to haul in the monster out in the deep blue sea. After what could be hours, they bring the beastly fish up to the boat, hook it with the gaff, and pull it on board.

When I retired from the military, our squadron decided to put together a fishing trip. Eight of us signed up and we chartered a boat. On the morning we arrived and boarded, I was concerned about the fishing order (you will be exposed to how competitive I am throughout this book!). In order to avoid any confusion, I proposed putting eight numbered pieces of paper into a hat and draw for who gets into the chair first. I drew last so that there would be no perception of impropriety. I drew the number one position.

After several hours of droning on the high seas (with a couple of my buddies feeding the fish their breakfast) we finally got the "Fish on!" yell and I climbed into the chair. Awesome – It was a Striped Marlin and put on a great jumping show for us. It was not huge and I managed to land it in less than half an hour. Unfortunately for everyone else on board, that was the only strike all day. People accuse me of being a very lucky fisherman.

Another style of fishing is with a fly rod. I am sure you can picture the beautiful backdrop of a Montana mountain range with a fly fisherman in the foreground. He is whipping his fly rod back and forth, eventually laying the fly slightly up river from a little eddy. He hopes the fly floats right over where he thinks his trout is lurking. I have only practiced this type of fishing, but my dad became very good at it in Oregon.

I am also sure you can picture a sleek bass boat, slowly trolling along a lily-lined lake. The angler casts his lures with precision accuracy, placing them between the reeds, lilies, or branches. They hope for the big lunker

Facing Page: The three Daubenspeck men slaying the Ahi on the Foxy Lady.

Chapter Intro Photo: Here is why the Tiger Shark was following us into the shallows.

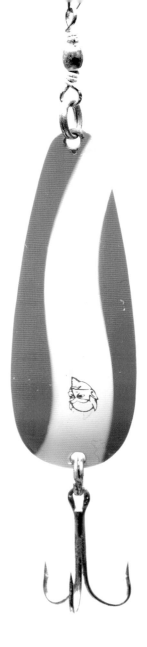

to come crashing through the surface, trying to throw the hook from out of its mouth. Many people actually make a good living competing in this style of fishing. This is what I cut my teeth on growing up. I still dream about doing more of it later in my life.

You may have been exposed to all of these, and other fishing styles, but you may not be very familiar with my favorite method, called freediving. Freediving is normally done in salt water, but has started to happen in fresh water settings. It involves snorkeling of sorts, with no other diving apparatus, like SCUBA gear. You get one breath of air to work with, and that is it. I am typically adorned in my camouflage suit with mask, snorkel, fins, knife, and speargun. You need to have a partner with you, because passing out on one breath of air while pursuing a fish, is a real possibility and not a good thing. I have too much to still accomplish.

Safety is my main concern, so my friend, Mark, and I went to Kona to take a freediving course to better our skills. David Blaine went through this same course before he tried his world record breath hold on live TV.

We spent four days learning about breathing physiology and practiced increasing our breath holding capacity in a pool for three days. Mark and I actually did quite well at this. On our final day of pool practice, we gathered to compete. They said it was not a competition. They must have been out of their mind.

Anyway, Mark and I paired up after we received instructions on how it would proceed. After doing our "breathing up" exercises, we would finally place our head down in the water, with our partner next to our side with a hand on our back. We coordinated signals; the one with their head in the water would acknowledge hearing the one monitoring the time by raising their hand slightly under water. We decided to break with that form and only move our finger so that less energy would be expended. The monitor would call out times over us and we could easily hear, even with our heads submerged. I was anxious to do this and super curious to see how well I would do.

In the first two minutes, only the 30-second signal was given. After that, it would be more frequent, getting to every five seconds. I passed the three-minute signal and everything was going swimmingly (ha!). And I even remember passing the four and a half minute call amazed at myself. At that point, the instructors came over because I was one of the only ones with my head still in the water. I approached the five minute mark and knew I was about to be done, but I could hear them on the pool deck talking to Mark, asking if I had signaled or not. There was no time for him to explain we had changed up our signaling, so when the 5:15 hit, they pulled my head out of the water. That was mildly upsetting. I was convinced I had a little more time left in me, but they were all convinced I was on the edge of passing out. I must mention that Mark would die before he let me better him on the breath hold, so he also made it to 5:15! I am sure he only stopped there in magnanimity.

For the depth training, we practiced our diving skills in one of the most beautiful settings on the planet, Pu'uhonua o Honaunau bay. Surrounded by colorful corals, we swam out, and dove for three days, with porpoises circling us from time to time. It does not get

Above: Joe Burke, Mark Button and Jeff Lee having a great day in NZ.

much cooler than that! On the last day, we would get three chances to successively dive for a personal best. Buy the end of the course, Mark and I dove down to 115 feet in the ocean, on one breath. What a great time!

I hope this gives you a little bit of an idea what freediving is as you read some of the stories that follow. When you hear the term "freediving" you can now imagine someone lying on the floor of the ocean, trying to disappear into the background, with speargun at the ready. And I hope you truly get some useful tips out of this book, so you can achieve all that God has for you in your life. Dive in!!!

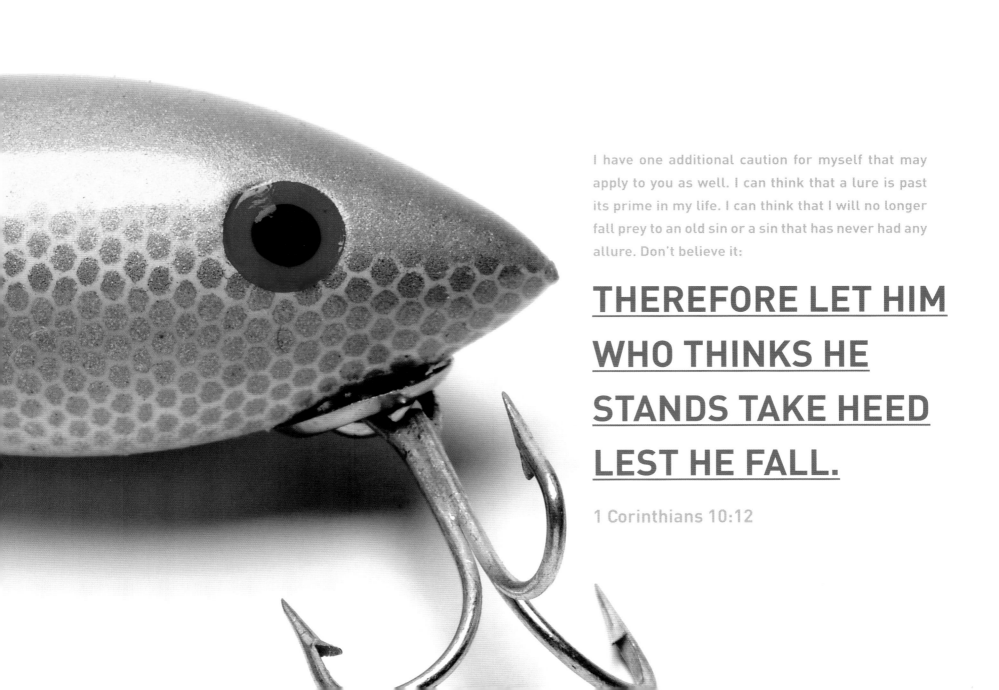

I have one additional caution for myself that may apply to you as well. I can think that a lure is past its prime in my life. I can think that I will no longer fall prey to an old sin or a sin that has never had any allure. Don't believe it:

THEREFORE LET HIM WHO THINKS HE STANDS TAKE HEED LEST HE FALL.

1 Corinthians 10:12

FISH PERSONALITIES

N THE FOLLOWING PAGES, I tell some fun stories of me catching, or spearing, fish in various settings with different gear. I will paint a picture of different fish personalities and how they might parallel human disposition throughout the tales. Some of the fish characteristics, and how they are attracted to lures, are very similar to how men fail to recognize the dangers that the enemy throws in front of us and how often we bite. By highlighting some of these differences, I hope to shine the light of truth on some of our own tendencies and possibly prevent us from ending up in the Fisherman's cooler. I break the fish personalities into six defined characteristics:

DO YOU SCHOOL? OR, ARE YOU MORE OF A LONER?

There are basically two main reasons that fish school. Most of them group together for protection. In large schools, enough can survive to mate and carry on the species. When the predators come in, they will confuse those predators by turning and moving as a group. Others, like Tuna and Dorado, travel in big groups to hunt. Working in unison, they surround a school of fish, keep them circled, and decimate them by teamwork.

ARE YOU TYPICALLY AGGRESSIVE OR ARE YOU SHY?

Are you the Barracuda, hunting down your prey? Or are you the Angel Fish, just hoping to mind your own business and keep out of the way?

ARE YOU TERRITORIAL OR DO YOU LIKE TO TRAVEL?

Do you stay close to home? Do you like deep water? Do you like to stay near the rock where you were born? Or do you want to travel the seven seas and see the world like a Marlin?

Above: Blessed to live in Paradise.

Facing Page: Jeff Schulte showing Grizzly's they are outmatched if you can't use your teeth or claws. Courtesy Jeff Schultz Photography

DO YOU HAVE A CURIOUS PERSONALITY OR ARE YOU PRETTY FOCUSED? Do you have set missions in life? Or do you like to explore other possibilities? Do you want to see what others are doing? Or what's going on next door?

DO YOU LIVE LIFE IN THE FAST LANE OR ARE YOU CONTENT TO JUST CRUISE? Does the scenery need to change pretty quickly? Or does life seem to move pretty slowly for you and you like it that way?

DO YOU LIKE SHINY OBJECTS (SHINY CARS, SHINY WATCHES, SHINY GUNS, SHINY TROPHIES, ETC.) or are you content without "stuff"? Are you "overly" focused on women? Do you put yourself in situations to attract women? Do you look for "target rich" environments? Are you prone to porn? This aspect applies in many of the categories.

After I put this manuscript out for review, I received feedback from a few people that I had included too many examples of fish descriptions and stories. At the same time, I had feedback that people loved them. My recommendation would be that once you get the point and are no longer entertained by the stories, move on to Section II. For those of you that enjoy them, thank you for reading them – I certainly enjoyed having the experience!

Facing Page: A beautifully colored Durham Ranger salmon fly (Wikimedia commons)

TIGER SHARK

TIGER SHARKS ARE THE SECOND most likely sharks to attack humans, behind the dreaded Great White, but it is still a very rare occurrence. The last confirmed fatality from a Tiger Shark was back in 2004 and there are only three other non-confirmed deaths since 2000. But, there is still a mystique about them and I would not recommend being careless around one. They have been found with license plates, oilcans, tires, and other shiny objects in their stomachs, so my partners and I are very careful if one is around when we are spearfishing.

I seem to be more of a Tiger Shark attractant than most people. I have lost count of how many times they have come around me while spearfishing in the deeper water. I even had one come very close when I was reef fishing with three other guys. We had a lot of fish and the smell had obviously brought it in to the shallows.

Sharks in general are pretty easy to read with their body language. I have gotten more and more comfortable around them as I have seen their behavior in different situations. When a shark is getting agitated or aggressive, it starts to hump its back a little more, like my man-eating Fox Terrier. It will also start to move its pectoral fins from a horizontal position to being lowered at an angle so that it can turn more effectively when it darts forward. The last indication, is that it starts to swim a little more erratically, instead of in smooth, predictable lines.

I have come across many Tiger Sharks on land. When I was growing up in elementary school, I would watch Steve Palmer, Eddie Ahrens, Tim Russell and Guy Hudson circle their prey after school. Why do I remember their names from the sixth grade after all of these years? Because they were Tiger Sharks. They could smell weakness and injury. They would come out of nowhere and start circling, looking for an opening. Sometimes, even I was their quarry. But, I don't remember them singling me out after I threw a large piece of asphalt into the back of Steve's head. Even a big shark will leave when you poke it in the side with a spear...

|||||||||||||||||||||||||||||||||||||

Tends to be a loner, does not school

Very aggressive

Usually mid-water, but can go either way

Always looking for a meal

Pretty slow - most of the time

Will eat just about anything, and I mean anything!

Facing Page: Tiger Sharks are some of the most beautiful fish as the sun dances off of their stripes in clear water.

KING SALMON

WHEN I WAS A TEENAGER, I was lucky enough to travel to one of the fishing capitals of the world, Alaska. It was a legitimate smorgasbord for the fish enthusiast. I fished for Sea Bass and Halibut in the ocean, but the fresh water fishing offered up the most expansive opportunities for me. The plethora of lakes and rivers throughout the state presented an astronomical variety of fish to choose from and I begged my mom and dad to stop at every turn of the road. The map that I was following was a fishing map and it would spell out what kinds of fish were in the bodies of water as we travelled along. I did manage to get a few stops along the way and gladly fished for Grayling, Rainbow Trout, Silver Salmon, Muskellunge, Pike, and King Salmon, just to mention a few. Towards the end of our vacation, I also got to go on a fishing expedition where the Susitna and Deshka Rivers come together and then travel up to the shallows where the Kings spawn.

Chinook, or King Salmon, are the biggest member of the Salmon family. They can reach a length of 58 inches and weigh as much as 130 pounds, but typically are less than half that size when spawning as adults. You have probably seen countless films of them jumping and splashing up rivers, being eaten by bears and eagles, as they single mindedly and relentlessly swam to their goal. They headed from the ocean, where they grew up, back to the shallow waters of a baby river where they were born to lay and fertilize their own eggs.

Because the King Salmon were spawning while I was there, it was illegal to keep anything that was bigger than 20 inches. I never caught anything small enough to keep. One time, I had a fish that was close and when the Park Ranger came over to check on me, he found that it was 22 inches and I had to let it go. The Ranger was very upset with me when I let the fish go without reviving it appropriately, and it sank upside down to the bottom. I am sure it was fine, but I was almost fined for my lack of fish care.

On the other end of the spectrum, I was able to watch a fisherman go up and down the river, chasing a huge King that he had managed to hook. When he eventually

Above: Jeff Schulte with a monster up in Alaska.

Facing Page: Gerry Freeman knows how to catch these beauties up in Canada.

IIIIIIIIIIIIIIIIIIIIIIIIIIIIIIIIII

Loves shiny objects and
other food when spawning

Runs in huge schools,
very social

Travels far, deep water
then shallow up the river

Medium speed

Neither Docile or
aggressive

Focused on spawning,
eats for energy along
the way

got the fish up to the boat, there was a tape measure glued to the side of the boat. That kept him from having to hoist the fish inside the boat to see how big it was. I pulled alongside, so that I could see for myself the size, and it measured a whopping 54 inches. I could only imagine hooking something so large, but I had my chance shortly after that.

As usual, I could not get enough fishing, so when the two adults I was with decided they were going to take an afternoon nap, I asked them if I could take the boat out by myself and fish some more. I don't know what they were thinking because they gave me the go ahead to do it.

Once I got out into the center of the river, I started casting my spinner bait with the red balls on it that was supposed to look like Salmon eggs. I also sat back and watched the cat and mouse game between the fishermen and the Game Warden that went on every day. Poaching is a big problem and with the amount of people doing it, along with their technology, the Warden could not have much of an impact. But, he tried nonetheless.

030

I would watch a plane go flying over the top of us, headed up the river to pick up the fish, and then the Warden would head up the river in his jet boat to go try and catch them. As he would leave, a "fisherman" in one of the boats would radio to the poachers as to what the Warden was doing. Not long thereafter, the plane would fly out, having picked up their booty and the Warden would come back to start all over again chasing the other way. Even the men I was with were poaching fish in some capacity or another.

As the game played on, a boat came over and the fishermen asked if I had any mosquito repellant that I could spare. What you need to realize is that the mosquitos up there are huge and unmerciful, so you always carry bottles and bottles of it with you. People joke that they are the state bird, because they are so big. And any square centimeter that is not covered in repellant is going to get unmercifully attacked. I did indeed have three bottles I could share and so I tossed one over to the very thankful crew. They, in turn, tossed over a sliver of Salmon roe as thanks. I then cut it into three chunks and changed out my lure for a treble hook.

After I got situated, I proceeded towards the bank and cast the roe about three feet from shore.

I don't even think it had time to settle to the bottom before my line went taught and audibly ripped through the water. The fish bolted upstream and took line at an unbelievable pace. As I saw the first half of the spool disappear, it was quite obvious that I needed to chase this beast up the river. Holding my rod high, I desperately got the motor started, steered the right way, and started reeling. I was beaming with pride as I pursued the big King past other boats with them encouraging me along the way. I figured out it is very hard to steer a boat in the right direction and also keep the line taught. As you might have already guessed, I was unsuccessful in doing just that and the big red monster went on to produce hundreds of little Salmon for future generations. I gave the other chunks of roe a chance, but it was not meant to be and I soon flew out on a little Piper Cub. I saw brown and black bears, beavers and bald eagles, and a female moose and her baby closer than I should have, but that fishing trip will be one of the highlights of a great trip.

BLUEGILL

[Lepomis macrochirus]

BLUEGILL ARE MEMBERS of the Sunfish family and tend to inhabit slow moving rivers, lakes, and ponds east of the Rocky Mountains, but have been introduced worldwide. They tend to stay close to aquatic plants and stay in groups of 10 to 20 individuals. They will boldly defend their spawning areas, but are generally a mild-mannered fish.

When I was living in Germany, I chose to have our family live on a farm about 30 minutes away from the Air Force base. I did not want to live in "little America", but wanted to be immersed in the local culture as I had growing up. I made friends with my landlord and I loved to practice my language skills with him. When I had a chance, I would find him on the farm and start talking about what he was doing and about his life. He was about 70 years old and ran the operations for the 40 milking cows, the cornfields, and the brewing of the potato schnapps. He also had quite a few rental properties, which he liked to rent to the military clientele. He had several irons in the fire at any one time, depending on the season.

He had a huge three-story house where they, his sister-in-law, and daughter and son-in-law lived. He started working early every day and worked until the sun went down. He worked a little less on Sundays, rarely left the farm, family members would visit on weekends, and he never ever went on vacation. We would meet at the pub, connected to the village fire station, every so often and make idle chat.

I would look at his life and be amazed, wondering how anyone could be so predictable and routine, without going crazy. But, he enjoyed his life and had no desire for it to be any different.

I could not understand his life any more than an Ono can understand a Bluegill...

||||||||||||||||||||||||||||||||||||

Moderately aggressive when spawning

Very social, family groupings

Stays close to shore, territorial at times

Neither focused or curious

Mostly stationary in a small area

Does not care about shiny objects

Facing Page: A nice fat Alabama Bluegill destined for the pan fry. (Wikipedia)

033

CATFISH

CATFISH HAVE SUCH a diverse family. They can be as large as the Mekong Giant Catfish, which holds the Guinness Book of World Records as the largest freshwater fish, down to something small that could be in your home fish tank. They are named from their obvious, sensitive barbels around their mouth, making them very perceptive to the environment around them, even in the dark or murky waters.

Catfish are normally loners, but will congregate in groups by circumstance. They do not like to travel very far from shore. Lately, they have become famous for their aggressive protective behavior regarding their eggs. They will inhabit holes in riverbanks or small caves, where they lay their eggs, and then protect them with a fury. Anything that tries to come into the hole will be fiercely rejected or bitten, which has popularized "Noodling". Noodling is the trick of sticking your hand into a catfish hole, whereby, the catfish bites it, and the person grabs the catfish by its mouth and pulls it out of the hole. Not for the faint of heart, but apparently entertaining TV fare.

I have never gone Noodling, but have fished for several different species, both in fresh and saltwater. They are very tasty critters and very popular all across the country. Mostly slow moving scavengers, they will eat just about anything that is presented on a hook, but sometimes will even take a lure.

As I am writing this book, I feel a little like a catfish. I have been "holed up" for quite a while and have not been out doing anything adventurous lately. I am trying to connect with my sensitive and perceptive side and write some of my thoughts down, but sometimes I feel like I am blindly making my way through muddy waters. In a way, this is deep water for me...

Tends to be more of a loner, does not school

Moderately aggressive when spawning, protective of young

Stays close to shore

Prone to overeating

Pretty slow most of the time

Will eat about anything

Facing Page: Larysa Switlyk star of NBC's Larysa Unleashed with a Red-Tailed Catfish in Thailand.

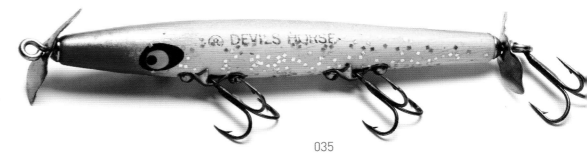

O TASTE AND SEE THAT THE LORD IS GOOD: BLESSED IS THE MAN THAT TRUSTETH IN HIM.

Psalms 34:8

GIANT TREVALLY

S HOOTING MY FIRST GIANT TREVALLY, or Ulua in Hawaiian, is where my passion for hunting big fish began. I had caught big game fish from a boat, but spear fishing is literally a different ballgame. I will let my son's account of one of our outings tell the tale. It was published in Hawaii Skin Diver magazine with a great picture of us with our trophy fish.

BLESSED *I heard the faint sound of his voice through the waterlogged hood of my wetsuit. A tone of boredom carried across the rippling ocean. I saw the lame facial expression. "You ready to head in?"*

More than an hour of swimming had brought us thus far, to no reward. It was only my desperation that brought me to say; "I'm okay," leaving the decision to him.

I was hardly surprised when he said, "Let's swim out this way for a while," as he pointed out in front of us, slightly to the left. At this, we both submerged back into the endless sea, and I began to follow the thousands of miniscule bubbles given off from my father's long Esclapez fins. They briefly breached the surface and then sank back down, propelling him effortlessly forward.

Below the surface was another world, as if the glassy water was a portal from Earth to a distant place in the far recesses of the universe. Looking up was like seeing a rippling blur of our faraway home. In a way, however, this was our home. For the three to four hours that we ventured in this vast expanse, it was like nothing else existed, nothing else mattered. All the worries of life were no longer alive in our minds. All that now remained were God, my dad, and me. Peace existed.

My gaze searched the rough bed of coral, rock and sand. Small fish scoured the bottom for food and shelter. The world around me soon became a blur as I became unfocused and my mind drifted off, imagining the action that should be happening. In this world, Uku and Omilu circled around abundantly.

Occasionally a fish, slightly larger than the rest, would swim by along the bottom, but we would take little notice. To us, these waters were filled only with an unquenchable thirst for greater life, something larger than the common 10-inch fish that no longer satisfied us.

I trained my eyes on the bottom, now around eight fathoms below. I could just barely make out the white dots of a Spotted Eagle Ray.

Above: Jon Barretto winning another tournament with his mad skills.

Facing Page: My face was cramping from big smiles as I swam in with this big boy!

Previous Spread: Kimi Werner showing us all how it's done.

IIIIIIIIIIIIIIIIIIIIIIIIIIII

Very prone to shiny objects

Mid to deep reef fish, moderate traveller

Runs alone or with a few others, in uncommon cases found in large schools

Aggressive

Usually hunting, but sometimes resting in "Ulua holes"

Slow hunter, but very fast when feeding

Facing Page: Ulua like to follow Spotted Eagle Rays and eat what the rays scare up.

I lifted my head and dully stated, "There's an Eagle Ray down there."

He thought little of it and continued on. I decided to dive down and take a look.

My mask had barely plunged down when I noticed something. This ray seemed to have two tails. When I made out what this tail was, I thought, No, it can't be. With speed barely possible underwater, I turned and surfaced.

I shouted, "Dad! There's an Ulua under that Eagle Ray!" After three quick breaths, he submerged. Moving like a missile diving from the sky, he shot through the clouds and, with a few kicks, angled towards the bottom. I watched as he straightened out his body and used his negative buoyancy to glide toward the bottom.

Thoughts were flying by at a thousand miles a minute. What if he misses? Is this really happening? That's a big fish. Can he get it? I was in a state of disbelief. At the same time, however, I was praying. God, please help him to get this fish.

My heart throbbed with adrenaline. Its rhythmic beating was far from its normal rate. Every inch of my father's descent increased it that much more.

Now, everything was in slow motion. He drifted down, down, down. His gun was now stretched out in front of him, ready to fire. His fins controlled the angle of his descent as he began to accelerate.

Click! WZZZZZZZZZZZZ!!! My mind sped back into real time as the Ulua shot off with the 65inch spear newly wedged into its body. It was a good shot, and the spear held fast as the fish rapidly took line from my dad's reel.

The reel's drag set in, and the fish began to pull my dad down. He was forced to pull line out of the reel himself in order to get to the surface. The fish still fought hard, trying desperately to escape.

Adrenaline pumping through me led me to irrationality and I foolishly attempted to swim down and help pull on the line. I was immediately signaled to stop.

The fight went on. My heart was pounding even faster and harder than before, and I was sure that my dad's was too. I could almost hear a slight thumping in the water.

Finally, the fish began to lose the fight. My dad had managed to pull it nearly halfway to the surface. We both stared wide-eyed as it came nearer. We were seeing a

Hawaiian gargantuan. And, now, our moment of victory was approaching. It was ever so near, just feet away. Only a few more moments and it would be ours.

Then came the shark. Its light gray body moved in from the distance, only to settle and begin circling around our trophy. The blood was fresh, the vibrations very apparent. It intended to steal our prize.

The shark's presence ignited the fight once again. It pulled toward the bottom with new, uncontainable energy, and it once again pulled my dad toward the bottom. He briefly resurfaced and shouted, "Come grab my weight belt, quick!"

I swam over and grabbed it from him. I was immediately surprised. I had not measured in the fact that his weight belt was exactly that, a weight belt, and I began to sink. His weight belt, combined with the weight of mine, was pulling me down. I was expending a lot of energy, so I swam to the buoy we were dragging around. I was not sure how to put it on the buoy, but I was tired. I was losing willpower and the thought of dropping the weight belt crossed my mind more than once. I looked down and noticed that I had also floated into deeper water. Fear was starting to run through me. Once again I began to pray.

Just as I managed to get the weight belt onto the buoy, I heard, "Just drop it and let's get out of here!"

"I got it," I replied and began to make my way back towards him. Once I got to him, he had the fish up and had wedged his hands in its gills, to stabilize it.

He told me to grab all of the gear, and we began our long, 45 minute, trek back to land. The current was against us. I constantly looked at the fish that my dad was carrying. We both wore wide smiles. I constantly gave him the thumbs up, showing my joy in this catch.

As we approached the beach, we happened to end up right in front of a crowd having a Labor Day party. A noise came from the crowd as we came out of the water. Then, as my dad thrust the fish around to display it broadside to them, an even louder cheer erupted. Amazement sounded as we dragged the fish through the water, its weight too great to carry on land. We had been blessed.

—Carter Daubenspeck

Above: Kevin Sakuda with his 118lb Ulua. Hammerhead packs a punch!

Facing Page: Justin Abilla with his 92lb Ulua in front of the Haleiwa bridge.

PARROTFISH

[Scarus rubroviolaceus]

PARROTFISH, OR UHU IN HAWAIIAN, are fascinating fish. They are named after the fact that their teeth are fused together and formed on the outside of their jaw in the shape of a "beak" which resembles a parrot. They feed on the algae on coral and the coral itself. In the process, they make "sand" as the coral bits eventually pass through them and are washed up onto our beaches. So as you walk along the beach and it comfortably washes between your toes, remember it was previously fish pooh.

Another fascinating aspect of Parrotfish is that they are sequential hermaphrodites, meaning that most of them are born females and then later change to males. There is only one, out of the approximate 90 species, that does not change in its life cycle. It is all very complex, but interesting to study.

In Hawaii, we have several species, most of which are very tasty fare and are famous at family parties. They do not take bait, so the only way to get them is by netting and spearfishing. And they are quite interesting to hunt.

At night, Uhu sleep in crevices and caves and they "spin" a net around themselves to shield their smell from predators. They actually form this cocoon by emitting mucous from their mouth as they are falling asleep. All of this makes them very easy to hunt at night if you know where they sleep. It is a very different story during the day, however.

Many of the species run around in harems, as they are called. There is usually a dominant male and a few dominant females, with a bunch of other females in various stages of growth following along. Of course, I like to go after the larger males for two reasons. One reason is because they are large, colorful and hard to get. The other reason is biological. When the dominant male

|||||||||||||||||||||||||||||||||

Mid-water fish, does not travel far

Docile, but territorial

Runs in harems, very social

Focused on eating coral

Tends to be slow

Not attracted to lures or bait

Above: Carter with his catch for the day.

Facing Page: All smiles for sunny days, calm seas and light winds. It doesn't get much better.

045

is taken out, one of the dominant females will change sex to take his place, and there is less impact on the life cycle. Okay, that second reason is so low on the totem pole, but makes my tree hugger friends feel better.

Successful hunting of Uhu usually involves a few strategies. The first is surprise. If you come upon them when cruising the reef, you better shoot quickly because they scare easily and will bolt along with the whole harem. The second is to appeal to their curiosity and hunger. As I will go into later, when lying on the bottom of the reef, you can scratch the rocks and imitate the sound of the fish feeding. That may bring them into range for a shot if you are lucky. Finally, you can appeal to their territorial sense. Many times, the dominant males will not want you to be around so they will start acting aggressive with you. They will come closer and start bouncing up and down, speeding up and slowing down, while swimming away and then coming back. Before they figure out that you don't matter, get a shot off. And make sure it is a good one, because they have very big and very hard scales. Because of that, spears frequently just bounce off and make you wonder about your aim.

Facing Page: Ray Arney and his boy Gabriel with their Star-Eye Parrots.

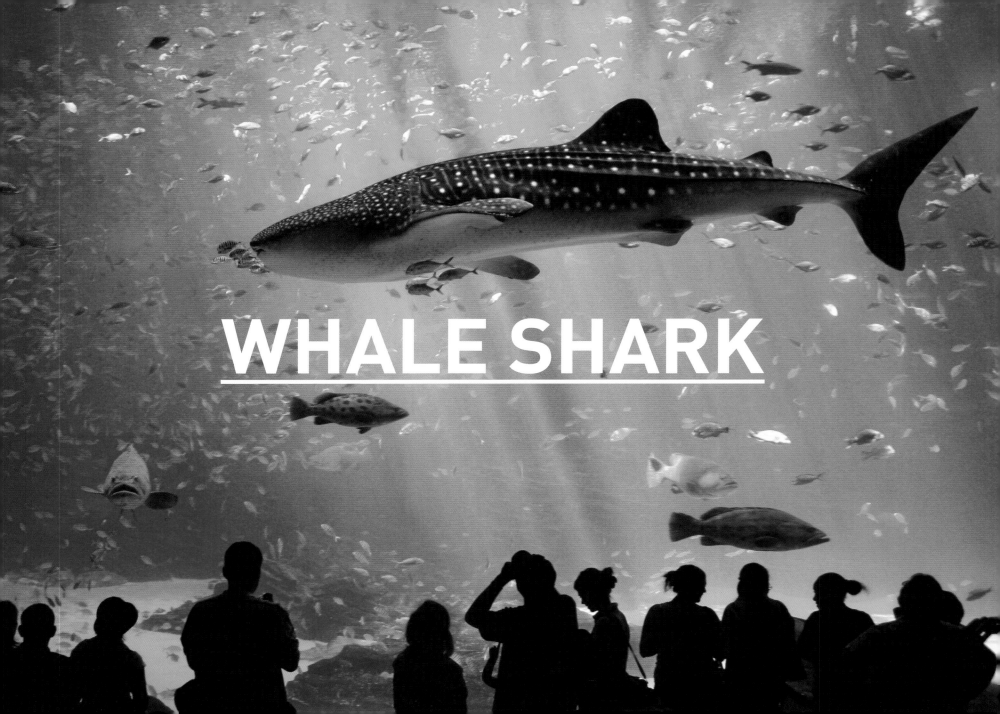

WHALE SHARK

[Rhincodon typus]

I AM NOT SURE IF JONAH SAW IT FIRST, or if I did. It did not really matter at the time. We both brought our guns to the front and swam up close to each other in a defensive position. As it approached through the murk in the distance, it looked like the biggest Tiger Shark we had encountered to date. The closer it got, however, we noticed it did not seem to be swimming in the same pattern as our normal "friend" that visited from time to time.

Turned out it was an almost exact opposite of our normal visitor. It was a whale shark on its calm, curious, lengthy journey, searching for plankton. It was a much more rare family member of the sharks that we were normally used to, but just as exciting, if not more. They are the largest non-mammals on the planet and can be over 40 feet in length and weigh over 50,000 pounds. This one was a juvenile and looked to be no more than 15 feet long.

Once we figured out what it was, it was time to get as many Hollywood shots as possible. On the first pass, Jonah grabbed hold for the first attempt at video,

and then it circled around for pass number two. I disconnected my camera from my gun and got ready. As it came in again, I jumped on and had one of the rides of my life, just wishing I had taken a deeper breath before our descent. It soon had enough fun with us and took a dive for the deep. Once again, it confirmed that you just never know what will show up on a Blue Water dive and it was a great experience for the both of us...

Loner, does not school

Very docile, but looks intimidating

Travels far, deeper water

Very curious

Would not hurt a flea, moves very slowly

Does not care for shiny objects

Above: Jonah later chastised me for the Hollywood shot as I rode the whale shark.

Facing Page: Georgia Aquarium.

WAHOO

ONE OF THE BEST PARTNERS I have for Blue Water hunting is, coincidentally, named Jonah. We can spend all day out in the wild blue yonder, floating along, and we rarely get tired of it. Part of the reason is because you never know what can show up at any time and we love seeing God's creation. In Hawaii, I have seen Manta Rays, Whales, Spotted Eagle Rays, Tuna, Whale Sharks, and Dolphins just to name a few of the magnificent creatures. I have even seen enormous Blue Whales from a helicopter. Of course, the other reason we don't get tired of it is because we love to hunt Wahoo. In Hawaii, they are called Ono and they are one of the best tasting game fish on the planet. In fact, in Hawaiian, the word "Ono" means delicious. Most big game fishermen try to catch them by trolling from boats, but my partner and I like to hunt them and land them with spear guns. They are not easy to catch, but once you learn a few tricks, you can improve your odds significantly.

Wahoo typically run in small numbers. They can be seen all alone from time to time and on rare occasion, in large numbers. In our experience, they usually come in a group of from two to five. We like to refer to them as wolf packs, as they hunt the schools of Opelu, or Pacific Mackerel Scad, and look very menacing. They are very wary fish and it takes some skill to get them in close enough for a shot. We usually use a three-step process.

The first thing we do is palu, or chum, the water. Chumming is the process of throwing dead baitfish into the water. They can be whole, cut, or torn into pieces. This accomplishes several things for us. It puts a flavor, or smell, in the water, which can bring in all kinds of fish, and is an adventure in and of itself. As the smell travels down the current, anything that encounters the smell may come up current to see what has happened and if there is a meal to be had. Also, the bits and pieces drift down to the lower depths and bring up fish that might be lurking below. Doing this, we are able to bring in Mahi Mahi (Dorado), Ahi (Tuna), sharks, Uku (Green Job Fish), and Omilu (Blue-fin Trevally) to name a few of the fish we see.

Facing Page: Jonah taught me much of what I know about hunting Ono.

Facing Page: Chad Coppin with his first Ono. I think I gave him the fever!

The next part of the strategy, for Wahoo, is to put out what we call flashers. These are lines in the water with flashy pieces of metal attached hanging down about 30 feet below the surface. They are attached to the boat, or our floats, and bounce up and down in the wave action. This flashing in the water serves to simulate the shiny flashes of a school of baitfish. Once the Wahoo comes in range, due to the smell of the chum, the shine of the flashers will, hopefully, bring them in even closer. At that point, they may be close, but still probably not within shooting distance. To get them even closer, we may have to implement the last trick.

Wahoo are built for speed and programmed to launch at the shiny Opelu when the time is right, but they are very scared of humans. To get them to overlook our presence, I keep a common table knife, bent at an angle, in my foot booty. At the last moment, I pull out the knife and throw it off to one of my sides. The Wahoo will then be mesmerized by the tumbling, twirling knife, head towards it, and be distracted from me. That is the point at which I get my gun ready, lurch forward, and pull the trigger. If all goes well, my shaft will fly

straight and true through the silver missile and the action is on! More often than not, the Wahoo will then run at unbelievable speed with my bungee line and float attached. Hopefully, he runs out of energy and I can pull him in before he tears off of the line or is eaten by one of our big gray companions. Because Wahoo is such a hard fish to capture, and tastes so good, it is a highly prized catch and will bring many smiles and retelling of the tales.

I think the Wahoo is special, as it is one of my favorite fish, and I think it most lines up with my personality. I tend to run in small groups, if not by myself. I am moderately aggressive and I like to travel the deep water, far from home at times. I can be very focused, but I do have some curiosity at times. I like living a fast life, with lots of changes, and I am susceptible to shiny objects. I do think I am getting better at avoiding them in my old age. I am learning to swim away when confronted by other aggressive fish, but I still have my moments.

GREEN JOB FISH

MY GOOD FRIENDS and neighbors, Mark and Jeff, were the first ones to teach me how to hunt Hawaiian Ukus, or Green Job Fish, as they are known around the world. Uku is a medium to deep reef fish, and they are one of my favorite fish to eat. They are typically between a few pounds, but can be up to 10 or 20 pounds when you see them cruising below you. My friend, Jon, from Kauai has the current record in Hawaii at 31 pounds. He is an animal and quite successful at hunting Uku.

Ukus are a predator fish, but they don't really hunt in the open waters. They like to follow the Weke, or Goat Fish, and hope that they scare something up when they are foraging. If you are fishing, you can get them with flashy lures or you can also get them with live or even dead bait. We, on the other hand, like to hunt them with spear guns, but they are very smart. They are very wary, but fortunately for us, they have one very bad weakness – they are a curious species.

Because they follow rays and Weke looking for pop-up prey, the best way to get them to come in close is to act like a big ray or bottom feeder. I will always remember shooting my first Uku on the North Shore of Oahu. We were hunting in about 20 or 30 feet of water looking for Omliu (Trevally), Uhu (Parrot Fish), Kumu (Saddleback Goat Fish) and Uku. As we scanned the bottom, we came upon a large open area of sand, and I decided to drop to the bottom and see what was around.

I took a few preparatory breaths and headed to the bottom. As I leveled off, I relaxed on the bottom and began my survey around me. I looked behind me and, there in the distance, I could see an Uku looking my direction. I took my friend's advice and started acting like a big ray. Grabbing hands full of sand, I started tossing them up in the water as if I was searching for buried prey. Sure enough, the Uku could not resist the urge and headed my way for a meal. Within seconds, it came into range; I lifted my gun and pulled the trigger. Fresh sashimi was now on the menu. It felt great to bag my first Uku and know how to lure these desirable game fish.

|||||||||||||||||||||||||||||||||||||

Medium speed, but can move quickly when eating

Moderately aggressive when feeding, otherwise shy

Neither close to shore or deep water

Shy but very curious when feeding

Likes shiny objects and food

Tends to be more of a loner, does not school

Facing Page: One of the only times my fish was bigger than Mark's.

LARGEMOUTH BASS

A 1965 CHEVY CAPRICE towing a Coleman pop-up camper with a Sears boat on top. A great picture burned deep into my memory banks. That is how the best camping and fishing trips started as I was growing up. We would head off to places like Roosevelt Lake or Apache Lake, but my favorite was going to Lake Patagonia.

We went there so many times, we knew the lake backwards and forwards. We had our favorite spots that we went back to time after time, like the rocky cliffs across and to the left and the reed beds to the right. Largemouth bass was our quarry and my dad always had the tackle box full of every imaginable lure. He had crank baits with huge lips and bombers for the deep areas. He had Big-Os, Rapalas, Spinners, Lazy Ikes and everything else under the sun for the mid-water realm. And he had Poppers, Jitterbugs, plastic worms and fake frogs for the reeds and lily pads. I can't even remember all the lures, but I had my own favorites and they were the Big-Os for underwater and the Jitterbug was my lure of choice for top-water.

Because I could not get enough of fishing, sometimes I would head out by myself when my dad would take a breather. He liked to go out in the early morning and in the evening, but chose to sit out the afternoons back at the campsite. I will never forget one particular day. On that bright, sunny day, I decided to walk all the way to where the river fed in to the lake. It was more shallow and muddy, with lots of trees, bushes and reeds. Perfect for fishing, or just exploring if that was unproductive.

I remember finally getting to the other end of the lake and stepping down to the edge. There was a submerged log and this looked to be the perfect spot for a "Lunker".

Bass are impulse eaters. They will jump on a lure if it makes the right action or flashes the right way. But, if given enough time to examine the lure, they will reject it most of the time. There is only a moment of time to get the lure moving correctly if you want them to jump on it. As soon as the lure hits the water, you better be cranking it so the fish does not have time to think. That's what was running through my mind as I clipped on my big, white, handmade Jitterbug.

Facing Page: Comparing my teen shot with Carter's. I'm not competitive or anything.

Tends to be more of a
loner, does not school

Moderately aggressive,
territorial

Does not travel far,
stays close to shore
or protection

More focused than
curious

Normally moves slow
except to catch its prey

Loves shiny objects

Facing Page: Rick Owens showing me
how to relax in North Carolina.

My dad had made this Jitterbug out of a piece of wood and added the parts from a different Jitterbug. It was painted white and was about 3 times the size of a normal one. It ran low in the water and danced slowly and loudly over the surface. One of my favorite sayings is "Go big, or go home" and this one fit the bill. I got it ready and cast it out as far as I could past the log below.

Like I was supposed to, I got the lure moving back towards me right away. It gurgled and bobbed back and forth just right. As it approached the far end of the log, I saw the flash. A big daddy launched up and sucked that Jitterbug right down and ran for the bottom. I yanked and started reeling right away, but the bass came back up, flying out of the water, and threw the lure in the air. "AAARGH!!!" What a huge disappointment. I was immediately convinced it would have been the biggest bass I had ever caught. Of course, after I reeled in the lure, I decided to give it another try.

I tossed the lure back to the exact same place. I was sure the bass would have learned its lesson and would be nursing its wounds under the log. Luckily, I was wrong.

060

As the lure approached the log again, the flash came back with a vengeance. It once again sucked the lure in and headed for the bottom. This time I was going to set the hooks deep so it could not throw the lure again. The fight was on and it was not coming to the surface. My adrenaline was pumping and I was already envisioning the giant hanging on my wall. Unfortunately, it was not meant to be as my line snapped under the weight of the behemoth. I was crushed to lose such a big monster, and also lose my favorite lure. I waited to see if it would float back up to the surface, but I had no such luck. As I dejectedly headed back to camp, I added this one to my list of the big ones that got away. A great memory, nevertheless.

YELLOWFIN TUNA

[*Thunnus albacares*]

ONE OF THE APEX predators of the ocean is the Tuna, or Ahi as they are referred to here in Hawaii. They are big, sleek, fast and just downright beautiful. Not to mention, it is one of the highest priced fish on the menu because of the rarity and taste. Of course, that makes it an apex trophy catch for the fisherman. I have had the pleasure of catching Tuna on charter boats, but nothing matches the satisfaction of being able to land one with a spear gun. I had the chance of a lifetime opportunity to go to Mexico and hunt Yellow Fin Tuna with a couple friends and it is one of the highlights of my spear fishing hobby, so far.

I met my partner John in Honolulu and we headed to San Diego to meet up with his friend, Al. After a layover there, we continued on to our Mexican adventure. Our trip consisted of a week enjoying the sights and sounds and wonderful food of the local town. The focus, however, was the three days of spear fishing in the middle. Each day started with loading up the boat with all of our gear, which was formidable. We had the normal freediving gear, and on top of that we had the monster guns, bungee lines, and floats meant to secure and hold these beautiful beasts. Then we would watch as our guide and deck hands would cast throw nets to get our bait for the day. The first two days, we netted sardines and the third day we netted a big load of anchovies. That proved to be the bait of choice for Tuna.

After securing our bait, it was time to stand around, talk, and stare over the horizon as we motored out for almost two hours to our destination. Our rendezvous was a submerged mountain peak and a long bank where the ocean currents welled up, bringing plankton rich waters up for the baitfish and predators. The tops of these outcroppings were at about 60 to 80 feet and if you grabbed a breath and dove down, you could see huge schools of various jacks and snapper. In fact, at times the seabed looked like it was moving and you were dizzy, when it was really an enormous school of snapper swaying in the currents.

The first day, we jumped into the water and started to get acclimated to the conditions. I took some film of the

Above: A little Shibi action out on the North Shore of Oahu.

Facing Page: Shawn Masaki with a nice Ahi taken in La Paz, Mexico.

big schools of Pompano and surveyed the bottom. I was amazed to see a gigantic tuna swim directly underneath and literally could not believe my eyes. I was not ready at all and did not even swing my gun into position. I remember telling myself that this was way beyond what I imagined. Alas, the first day yielded no results in the cooler, but it was an amazing day, nonetheless.

Day two began at the same mountain peak, but after a couple hours we moved over to the submerged bank to see if our luck would change. Our system entailed getting a big zip-lok bag full of bait and tucking it into our weight belts and drifting in the current for about 30 minutes over the bank. Every few minutes, we would take out a handful and throw it in front of us. It would then slowly sink and spread out in the water. When the dispersion would get to about 30 feet, we would take a breath and swim down and wait as long as we could for some tuna to dart in. Eventually, we would reach the end of the bank and the boat would pick us up, take us to the far end, and we would start the whole process over again.

Our system was not working very well. We were each floating along like Lone Rangers, doing everything in isolation, and I was mildly frustrated that it was not the safest way to operate. I decided to swim over to where one of my "partners" was located and at least be in the vicinity of someone else. As I approached, I noticed a very long tentacle stretched out before me. The ocean was loaded with all kinds of jellyfish, which I was not used to, and they would startle me with their size from time to time. As I focused better on this tentacle, I noticed it was really Al's bungee line, so I looked up to see where he was. I saw him hanging on to his float as it was being pulled along. I realized he had a Tuna on the end of his line.

I hurried over to where he was headed and strained my eyes down into the deep, looking for the fish. I finally saw it and was completely amazed. It was huge! He obviously needed some help, so I swam in even closer. At that point, I took a breath and dove down to assess the situation. As I approached, I saw the spear had penetrated the side of the fish, but in the fight, it had pulled the shaft free to the point the flopper was only holding on to about an inch of skin. I quickly surfaced and yelled over for him not to pull very hard on the line and that it was barely holding. I then asked him if he wanted a back-up shot and he gave me the go-ahead to secure it.

I started breathing up and then filled my lungs. Pointing my gun in front of me, I started down and soon converged on the beast. I then paralleled the fish so I could get a perfect holding shot, which would hopefully end the fight as well, and pulled the trigger. I could immediately see it was a fatal blow and headed back to the surface to help haul it in.

At that point, the boat captain could tell something was up, so he headed over and idled up to the two of us with our tangled mess. With both of us wrangling the lines, we managed to finally pull it to the surface, secure it and hand it over to the deck hands. It was so big they had to stick the gaff in it to get it on board. We soon climbed aboard to start telling the tale from each other's perspective.

Turns out, the fish had a parasite in one eye and could only see clearly in one direction. It had glided past my friend without seeing him and he chased it for a very long time before being able to get in range for a shot. Because the shot was taken from such a distance, it had not completely penetrated to the other side for the flopper on the end of the spear to open and hold the fish. That was the reason it was hanging so precariously on a piece of skin and it was very lucky that I had come along when I did. The fish weighed in around 150 pounds and makes the perfect centerpiece for a great fish tale to be told over and over again.

I had an idea for day three. I proposed that we work more as a team and stay together. That way, we could each throw our handful of baitfish and then take turns diving down among the cloud. I must say, it was a great idea and we ended up getting four more Tuna that day, although none eclipsed the big boy from the day prior. I managed to bring in a 70 and a 90 pounder and I will never forget the sequence of events for one of them.

Floating along in somewhat of a triangle formation, we were each throwing our bait and dropping down on it in turns. On one particular drop, I noticed John was down pointing his gun at some quarry in the distance that I could not see. He eventually ran out of air and began to surface. As he did, he looked up to Al and I and flashed his two fingers signaling that there was a pair of Tuna roaming around. I looked over at Al to see if he was going to head down and he motioned for me to go down instead. I summarily breathed up and descended. Putting my gun in front of me, I surveyed the seascape to see if I could find what he was signaling about. I leveled off at about 30 feet and kept scanning.

Out of the green haze on my right, I saw them coming to cross my front. It ended up being two nice sized Tuna, quickly eating the bait. They were zipping from one piece to the next, like a giant connect the dot drawing. As they approached my left, I knew they were almost done and they turned to exit the stage back where they came from. I frantically tried to swing my gun to the right as fast as possible before they were gone. In a last ditch effort, I pushed the handle slightly left, to push

the tip to the right, and pulled the trigger. It was as if I could feel the shaft penetrate the Tuna. As the injured missile propelled down and to the right, the stainless shaft bent back viciously under the strain. The bungee stretched and my float came ripping through the water from behind. It was a good holding shot.

I shot to the surface and attempted to grab the bungee line before the float was out of reach. Putting the bands over my shoulder, I released my gun, grabbed the line and was towed along the surface. I had learned earlier not to fight the fish and let the float do what it was designed to do. If you tried to hold a Tuna from swimming down, you would lose badly. If you let the float wear the Tuna out, you win. Once it is apparent the fish is exhausted,

you can start pulling them in, hand over hand, clipping off three feet of bungee at a time. If the fish finds new energy, it does not really matter. It will still be fighting the float, although closer and closer each time another length of line is clipped off.

Using that method, we were able to successfully land the Tuna and we finished off the trip with a hugely successful haul. We had wrangled five big boys. I hope I can repeat a similar journey some day, but if not, I still have great memories of our successful adventure.

||||||||||||||||||||||||||||||||||||||||

Runs in huge schools, very social

Aggressive when feeding

Deep-water fish, travels very far

Focused on eating

Very fast

Very prone to shiny objects

Facing Page: I put the back-up shot into this 150lb beast for Al Hanson to get it on board

067

CLEANER WRASSE

[*Labroides phthirophagus*]

N HAWAII, there is a very beautiful Cleaner Fish, which are members of the wrasse family. They are brightly colored in neon purple, blue and yellow. They typically have an area under a ledge, or in a cave, where they set up their service stations and wait for their patients to come by for attention. The Cleaner Fish remove parasites and dead skin from their hosts and the little marine nurses lives off of those little bites of nutrition. In fact, they typically die in captivity because there are not enough parasites for them to survive off of. The other fish, even large carnivores, come by and make movements and body signals to relay that they are ready for cleaning. The Cleaner Fish will even enter their mouths and gills to remove the myriad parasites. The Cleaner Fish, therefore, get meals off of the other fish for survival and the infected fish benefits by having the parasites removed. It is a great and mutually beneficial symbiotic relationship. Just so everyone is aware, I live with a Cleaner Fish.

I had to put this one in here to pay tribute to my wife. My life would be incomplete without her.

Tends to be more of a loner or in pairs, does not school

Very docile

Homebody

Focused on helping others

Stationary, but bounces

Does not care about shiny objects

Left: The love of my life sharing good times with me.

Facing Page: Hawaiian Cleaner Wrasse working on a White Spotted Puffer (Wikipedia).

069

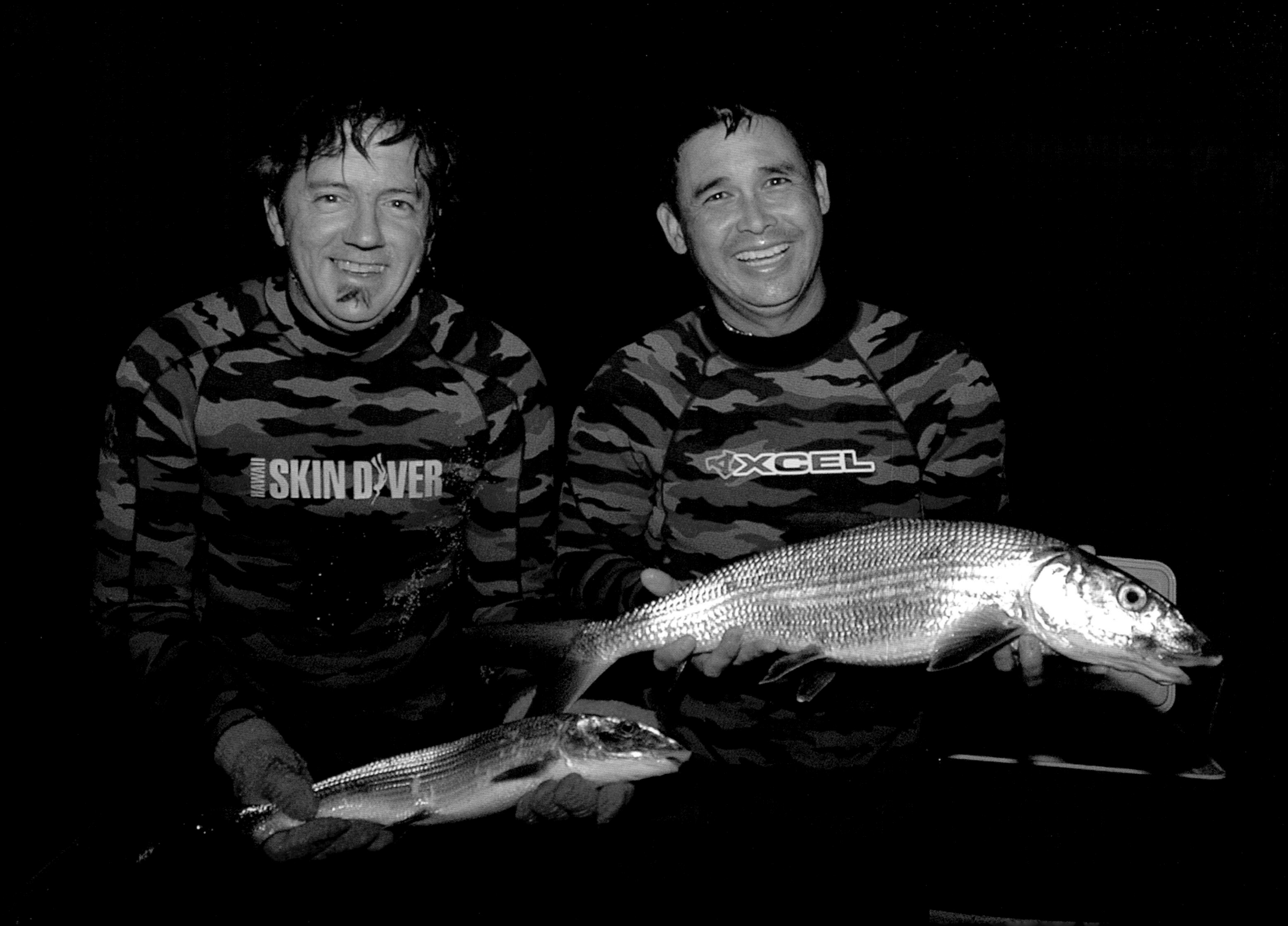

HAWAII SKIN DIVER
XCEL

SECTION ONE / CONCLUSIONS

AS MEN, I BELIEVE we typically have personality types that are very similar to fish in many ways. In particular, I believe that we mimic more of the predatory fish in our actions and pursuits. Because of many of those aspects, and our competitive nature, we are very susceptible to the lures that are thrown in front of us. I further believe that if we can acknowledge our traits, our tendencies, and more importantly our weaknesses, we can build appropriate and successful strategies to keep from being enticed by the enemy, and avoid being caught by the best fisherman out there.

Since there are 720 combinations for even the limited list of six characteristics that I mentioned, it would be a monumental task to find a fish for each and every profile that I listed. On the other hand, we can get a general idea of our personality by asking just a few questions. And what do we do with those answers? Let us examine and answer the questions of our schooling proclivities or whether we run alone. Maybe we need to have a few others around us to check our actions. Are we too aggressive, or do we let others run over us? Do we like adventure and running in the deep water, or are we supposed to stay closer to home and out of danger. Do we have an appropriate focus in our lives? Are we fulfilling what we are called to do or are we just floating along in the current of life? Are we living our lives too quickly? Are we taking the time to smell the roses along the way? Or, because of the pursuit of "things", are we ignoring that still small voice? Additionally, what is our "flashy" object or desire that can take us unknowingly out of our safety zone and into the dangerous waters? If you don't know, you are setting yourself up for failure, because the Fisherman probably knows better than you do.

Now, let's turn our attention to that Fisherman. Let's also examine the many lures he uses to catch you and me and the predator friends we swim with.

Above: Time to call it a day and head back in to Haleiwa Harbor.

Facing Page: Ray Arney and Brian Aki love to night fish out back.

071

The fisherman and his lures.

WHAT DOES THE FISHERMAN LOOK LIKE? AND WHAT DOES HE WANT?

I think that it is ultra-important to know that you are a target. You are a prize in the Kingdom. But, both sides are calling you. Do you want to be written in the book of life, or do you want to be hanging in the enemy's trophy room. One particular scripture makes it all very clear to me:

1 Peter 5:8

Be sober, be vigilant; because your adversary the devil walks about like a roaring lion, seeking whom he may devour.

Because we don't live in Africa, I might take a little liberty for this book and paraphrase it like this:

1 Peter 5:8 (Tackle Box version)

Be sober, be vigilant; because your adversary the devil casts about like a wise fisherman, seeking whom he may catch with his lures and devour.

John 10:10a (Tackle Box version)

"The Fisherman does not come except to steal, and to kill, and to destroy."

What makes it even harder is that the Fisherman and his helpers look so friendly. I imagine them looking like nice old fishermen, standing on the shore with big smiles on their faces, looking to help you out. Nothing could be farther from the truth as they are wolves in sheep's clothing:

2 Corinthians 11:13-15

For such are false apostles, deceitful workers, transforming themselves into apostles of Christ. And no wonder! For Satan himself transforms himself into an angel of light. Therefore, it is no great thing if his ministers also transform themselves into ministers of righteousness, whose end will be according to their works.

The bottom line is that the enemy wants your failure and will do whatever it takes to make that happen. He knows what entices you and attracts you. He knows that he needs to use a different lure at a different time of the day. He knows to use a different lure in different seasons of your life. And he knows you may not bite the first time that it comes by, so he is going to throw them

Above: Jeff Schulte showing off his Rainbow skills.

Facing Page: If you were an Ahi, could you resist these beautiful heads from Tsutomo Lures?

Early fishing lures were basically fish shaped pieces of wood with hooks attached. Fishermen have since added color, shiny spoons, propellers, noise making apparatus, and even lights. Fishermen will try almost anything to catch fish.

WHAT MAKES LURES ATTRACTIVE?

The objective of a lure is to be as authentic as possible. To accomplish that, there are two aspects that need to be addressed.

The first consideration is to make the lure look like the real thing. For fish, that means making it shine like it is supposed to. It means making it the same color as the bait, and probably the same size, as well.

The second consideration is to make the lure act just like the real thing. For fish, that means that it shakes the same way it is supposed to. If it is supposed to be a squid, it torpedoes through the water. If it is supposed to be a minnow, it wiggles in the water or goes back and forth the way they swim. It better crawl on the bottom

day in and day out, without fail. You better be vigilant and looking out for them, every minute of every day.

Fishing Lures have been around for as long as men saw that there were fish in the oceans, lakes, rivers and streams. I think fishing lures even predate the inventing of the wheel. It is just a natural progression for the lure to come before the boat, and the boat came before the trailer. Of course, the suburban was right after the wheel because you need one of those to haul the boat around. Anyway, fishing lures have constantly undergone continual changes and updates. As fishermen become better at knowing fish, they become better at manufacturing lures.

like a crayfish, jump on the surface like a frog, or float along like a mayfly. Whatever the case, if it looks as real as it can, it has a better chance of getting the fish to bite.

I want to, again, mention something that applies for both aspects of the lure. One sight that I have **never** seen is a fisherman walking up to the shoreline, or out on the dock, opening his box, selecting his lure, getting his rod ready, casting out in the water, reeling it in once, and then packing up and going home. When the fisherman is ready to fish, he fishes. Incessantly. Relentlessly. Sometimes neglecting the family and even neglecting themselves. The passion to catch fish may be an obsession that overshadows many other things. You need to know, the enemy is no less passionate about catching you.

Speaking of passion, before I took up spearfishing, I had my license to catch tropical fish. I would gear up with my fins, mask, snorkel, bait bucket, and net and head off to various shores of Oahu in search of a new and elusive prize catch. Time always stands still as you swim along and see all the beautiful sights under the

surface. Yellow Tangs dance between the coral fingers, Bird Wrasses dart into the cracks and crevices, and you may even see a Lauwiliwilihumuhumu'oi'oi, or the Long-nosed Butterfly Fish, swimming upside down under a ledge. You just never know what you might see or experience and it all goes by too quickly.

On one of my earlier forays into Kaneohe Bay, I left my wife and kids up on the shore and headed out on my expedition. After about five hours, I made my way back to shore and noticed my wife was walking down to the shore to meet me. I got in to the shallows, removed my fins and sloshed over to my wife, where she summarily told me "If you are ever gone for that long again, you will be walking home!" I learned to let her know how long I would be gone in the future and to set her expectations on the high side.

Above: If you really want to get your adrenaline going, shoot a fish in the vicinity of a few of these at the same time.

077

Above: Brian Aki showing off his prize Kumu.

Facing Page: Jeff Lee and I had a good day against the Mahi Mahi.

HOW CAN LURES BE ACCENTUATED?

As mentioned earlier, the object of a lure is to repeat reality. Besides looking and acting appropriately, one can accentuate fishing lures with at least two things: smell, and sound.

In the first section of the book, I talked about "flavoring" the water by chumming. This puts a smell in the water and is designed to get the fish in the mood to eat. It is kind of like driving down the Texas highway, past the giant BBQ joint, and you smell that wonderful sauce on that side of beef or pork and you want to turn around and go get some ribs, coleslaw and hush puppies. The best part is you don't get a spear in the head if you go get some.

The other way to get fish interested is by sounds that imitate feeding fish or fish in distress. When I am lying on the bottom of the reef, I will sometimes scratch the rocks with another rock, imitating the Parrot Fish chewing on the coral. It gets the other fish in the area excited. I know guys who will also strum the bands on

their reef guns, which creates a curious noise for some other kinds of fish. And a fish in distress will bring in a predator just like a whining rabbit will bring in a coyote. Sometimes I will slap my hand on the surface of the water and sometimes I will grunt like a small Jack Fish. The best example of this, which my son will never live down, was when we were reef hunting on the North Shore of Oahu.

We were cruising together in about 50 feet of water, when I saw a Yellow Spot Trevally, which had cornered his lunch in a crevice on the bottom. I decided to drop down on him and make him my lunch instead. As I sank down, closer and closer, I noticed that one of my ears was experiencing some pain. Because I was now so close, I ignored the pain and subsequently, felt cold water start trickling down my throat. I had popped my right eardrum and water was leaking through my Eustachian tube into my throat. I was totally disappointed with myself and, on top of that, I was now totally dizzy from the water in my ear. Since I had already done the damage, I decided to shoot the fish, even though I was upside down and my world was spinning. Maybe

Above: Mykal, Carter, and their friends honing their 3-prong skills back in the day.

not the greatest decision ever, but I made the shot and headed for the surface.

Once I surfaced, I hollered at my son that I had popped my eardrum and needed some help. He came over and began to assist me in dispatching the Trevally and untangling my line. As he held my gun, and I grabbed the Trevally, it started to grunt quite vociferously. At that point, I looked past my son and saw a Giant Trevally (and it was a giant!) coming to see if we were going to share our lunch with him. I motioned for my son to shoot it and he turned, leveled his gun, and pulled the trigger. Unfortunately for him, his safety was still on and the fish bolted for the deep. Why can't we just forget the ones that got away? I guess it makes us better.

HOW DO FISHERMEN CHOOSE LURES?

We went over some of this a little earlier, but there are several factors to look at. Fish feeding is regulated by internal and external forces and mostly at certain times of the day, although some will take advantage if food shows up at an opportune moment. That food will also present itself at different times, depending on what it is. Additionally, that particular food may not even be around, depending on what the season is. Let's look at each of these in greater detail.

Freshwater fish typically feed at set times of the day. They are more active and looking for food at those times. As I mentioned before, my dad liked to fish for bass very early in the morning and when the sun was going down. That was when bass were more likely to bite. I, on the other hand, had loads of energy, so I fished all day. That's why they call it "fishing" and not "catching" most of the time.

Saltwater fish also feed at different times of the day, but many of them are influenced by the tides, or other

THEREFORE SUBMIT TO GOD. RESIST THE DEVIL AND HE WILL FLEE FROM YOU.

James 4:7

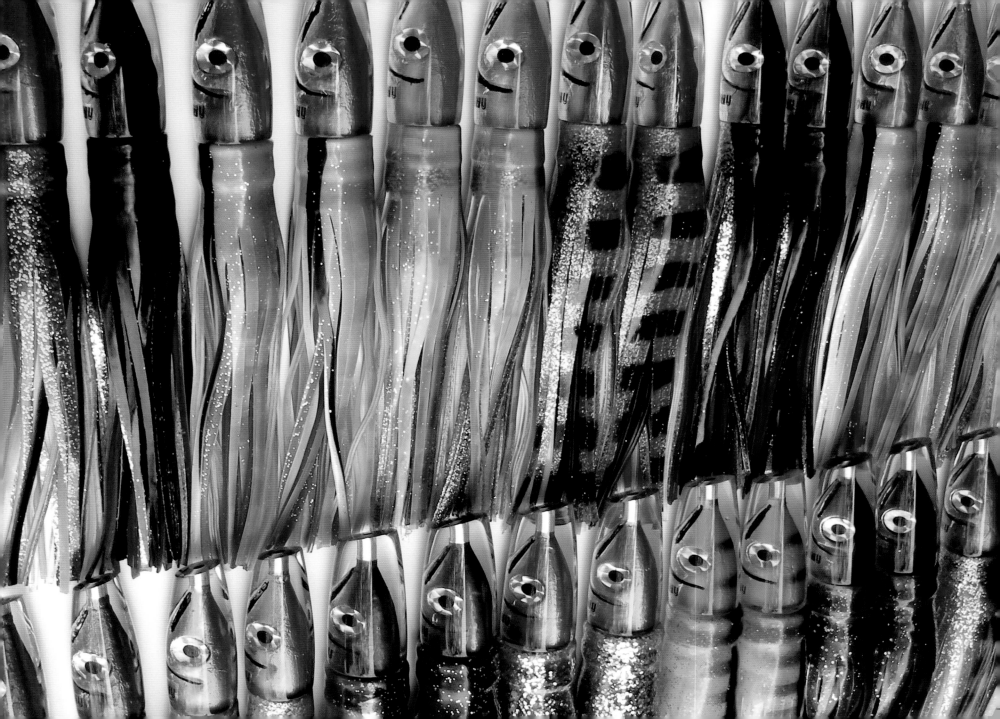

external the forces. The baitfish and the currents move differently, depending on the tides, so good fishermen are very knowledgeable about the tides – when they are low and when they are high. If you don't fish at the right times, you may not only be wasting time, you may be wasting gas and bait as well. Good fishermen don't like to waste either.

It also could be a waste of time throwing a spoon or flashy lure on a moonless night. With no reflections possible, the fish may know that minnows are not running at that time. They do, however, know that frogs are active at that time of night, so it may be better to throw a top-water, frog-mimicking lure and give it some nice, splashy pulls.

The seasons present different opportunities as well. For instance, out here in Hawaii, Oama (the smaller goat fish) come in close to shore around the August time frame. Consequently, the predators also come in close to shore to find them. The Oama will run in huge, dark schools up and down the coast. Sometimes, you can watch them start jumping in the air and splitting up as the predators dash in for a meal. That is a great time for the fisherman to throw an Oama, or an Oama-like lure, into the water. The feeding frenzy may give them the catch they are looking for.

All of this demonstrates the tactics used by fishermen to get fish in the mood to bite, get them in close enough to hook or spear, and finally get them to take the bait. Just like game fish, we can be put in the mood, brought in to the wrong environment, and lured to our demise. The Fisherman has many, many tactics to take advantage of the denial of our weaknesses or the overestimating of our strengths. I mentioned earlier that fishermen added color, shiny spoons, propellers, noise making apparatus, and even lights to their lures to enhance their fish catching skills and that they will try almost anything to catch fish. The Fisherman is the same way. He, on the other hand, has known the fish personalities since the beginning. He only changes the lures as the man changes his wants. An examination of the lures of man shines amazing light on how similar we can be to the unsuspecting fish.

Above: Ke-Ari Sumpter creating a little Alaska action while taking a break from school.

Facing Page: What color skirt would you wear to the dance?

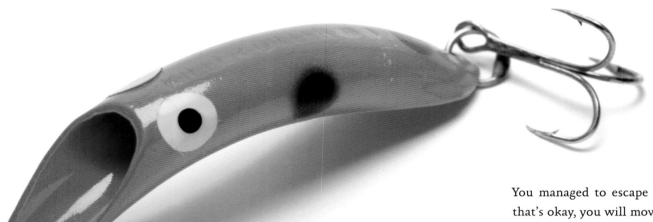

REMEMBER, THE FISHERMAN IS A KEEN CONSERVATIONIST.

The Fisherman is a true environmentalist in the fact that he is a staunch proponent of the catch and release program. He is perfectly happy to pull you up to the boat, gently lift you out of the water enough to pull the hook out of your mouth, revive you for a little bit, and release you back into the wild. Is it because he is such a loving and benevolent Fisherman? Not on your life. It is because he knows that you will now be that much more willing to bite a bigger lure later. Or, maybe he merely wants you to go out there and keep doing what you are already doing. You may even have assessed the situation and figured that it was not as bad as it could have been.

You managed to escape some dire circumstances, but that's okay, you will move on and make sure you never do anything like that again. The Fisherman knows better than that.

For example, if you have not set some very strict guidelines in dating before you get to that point, he is going to toss the lure of putting your hands where they don't belong. The Fisherman gently releases you to go back down to your watery hole with just a little pinhole in your lip. In fact, your other fish buddies even pat you on the back and encourage you to bite bigger and bigger lures. No worse for wear, you are soon back on the hunt and setting yourself up for failure in the future. If you are not careful and deliberate to put a hedge of protection around yourself, you will continue to be attracted to, and fall prey to, the varied and effective lures of the Fisherman. Let's look in more detail at each of these lures.

Above: Five Marlin in one day! Gerry and the boys know what they are doing!

WHAT DO THE LURES FOR MEN LOOK LIKE?

Just like on any given day, one particular tuna will bite on the bullet-head lure with the blue skirt, another tuna will prefer the bullet-head lure with the purple skirt. I don't even need to stretch my metaphors to be all too clear that different men will chase different color skirts, depending on how they woke up that morning. Every man has a different breaking point, a different set of weaknesses, and a different set of attractions that represent lures. My intention is to highlight six different lures that I believe represent the major areas of weakness for the vast majority of men:

ADVENTURE/FREEDOM   POWER/PRIDE

OVERINDULGING/EXCESS   SEX/LUST

ANGER/AGGRESSION   MONEY/TOYS

I think that if we can honestly assess each one of them, and the hold they can have in our lives, we can be much more capable of resisting them. And with God's power we can not only overcome the enemy, but he will also flee from us:

James 4:7
Therefore submit to God. Resist the devil and he will flee from you.

I have one additional caution for myself that may apply to you as well. I can think that a lure is past its prime in my life. I can think that I will no longer fall prey to an old sin or a sin that has never had any allure. Don't believe it:

1 Corinthians 10:12
Therefore let him who thinks he stands take heed lest he fall.

ADVENTURE/FREEDOM

A S I AM SITTING HERE writing this, I can see a clear example of how the free spirit can rule over a life. The waves are up and all across the horizon, there are countless surfers vying for position for the next set. I am not saying that every one of those guys or gals is irresponsible, but I know there are many out there that are dreaming of being the next Andy Irons or Kelly Slater. The lure of fame and fortune, or even just the next barrel at Pipeline, has caused many to give up on education and/or working towards a better job or family situation. Yes, every once in a while, someone hits the jackpot and lives the life of their dreams. Even as I write this, I have dreams of this book being quite successful and I question whether or not I should be focused on going out and selling the next house instead. It's a healthy mental argument, though, and I constantly measure it financially and spiritually, which I recommend for everyone (my wife helps me keep that in the healthy zone as well!).

In contrast, I have a friend who tested parachutes for a living. It wasn't much in terms of money, but the

freedom of his schedule and the disdain for a formal education, led him to go that route. He followed it up, however, with a license to fly helicopters and planes and always looked for ways to grow his business. He now travels the world doing airshows and competing in airplane races and has major sponsors working with him. It was a realistic approach to his desire for adventure and there ended up being a good balance.

As my youngest boy approaches the end of college, I am recommending for him not to jump straight into a full-time, seemingly responsible job with the pressures

Facing Page: It takes a lot of practice and skill to be able to surf cast with effectiveness and accuracy.

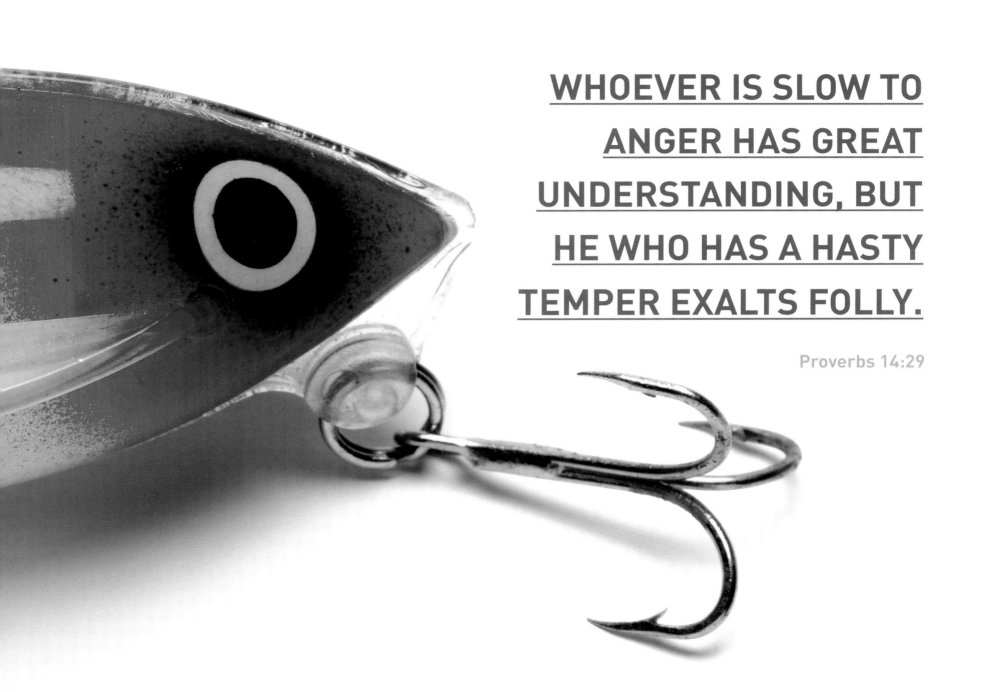

WHOEVER IS SLOW TO ANGER HAS GREAT UNDERSTANDING, BUT HE WHO HAS A HASTY TEMPER EXALTS FOLLY.

Proverbs 14:29

Facing Page:
Carter Daubenspeck,
Trevor Millar and Jay Schulte
cleaning up in beautiful Alaska.

associated with it. If there is not a balance to a life of work, the lure for adventure could pop-up later with devastating results. This is the proverbial mid-life crisis. I have had at least one of those! Balance and, more importantly, a genuine call on your life should be prayerfully and thoroughly examined from all angles. When you find the path that leads to your designed future, it may be difficult, but it will feel "right".

2 Thessalonians 3:10
For even when we were with you, we commanded you this: If anyone will not work, neither shall he eat.

The bottom line here is that there is balance between working and playing if you are going to be responsible to yourself and to others around you. Realistic expectations for both require a careful look at yourself and the world around you. I am even weighing all of this out as I write this book. Is it responsible for me to leave a lucrative real estate career and pursue speaking and writing? If that is what God is calling me to do, it would be wrong for me to resist that path.

POWER/PRIDE

POWER AND PRIDE is one of the trays in the enemy's tackle box that has my name on it in big, bold letters. Actually, I am listed on several of the trays, but this tray has a special section called "Awards and Trophies" and another section called "You are better than that guy" where my shiny and colorful lures are kept. I am a very competitive person and I like to beat people in just about every aspect of life. Of course, some of that competitive drive is healthy, like when I was a fighter jock. I better be able to kill the other guy in a dogfight or I will be the one being blown out of the sky. That same competitive spirit, however, in the family or workplace, might not be quite as healthy.

The proverbial bigger office, bigger paycheck, and bigger name have been the downfall of so many men. It has become cliché to mention that nobody, on their deathbed, expresses remorse, having spent too much time with their family and not enough time at the office. And many men have lost the dreams they envisioned for their families and the spiritual fruit in their lives by chasing the lures that are continually tossed in front of them. Inevitably, they gulp it down, and are pulled out of that little pond and thrown into the next pond up, with the bigger and bigger fish along the way. And so it goes, in pond after pond. They become so removed from the little pond with the fruitful dreams, and instead become the big fish, with the little dreams, that the fisherman desires.

Mark 4:19
"and the cares of this world, the deceitfulness of riches, and the desires for other things entering in choke the word, and it becomes unfruitful."

I recall years ago when God put an exclamation point on teaching me that I am quick to judge people. I still struggle with it every day, but I recognize it more often

Facing Page: A Yamashita rainbow of colors. What do you think will work today?

093

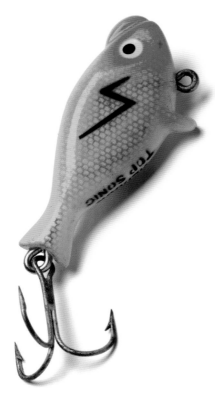

and try to change how I think. I was sitting in a Hawaii arena waiting for the Promise Keepers speaker to begin. This was the first time it was being held in Hawaii and I had been really looking forward to it. I had such a good time at the one held in the Hoosier Dome with 60,000 men, I was convinced I needed to come. That one had resulted in Julie and me changing which church we belonged to and pretty much changed a few of our foundational outlooks on denominations. Anyway, I was just sitting there biding my time until the event kicked off, listening to the two guys in front of me talk. I was overhearing the small talk and I determined that one of them was a chef and I think the other one was an artist. Based on my judgment, it did not seem to me that either one of them were Christians and I was wondering why they showed up to the event. I was still confounded to know why they came when the first speaker finally began.

The message was about judgment. I am not sure at which point in the message it hit me. It was like being hit in the head with the sledgehammer and it put a large dent in my self-image. At the end, I was totally convicted

and determined to change my thought process. Since God was going to help me along in that, He decided to have the speaker give an alter call and a call for some in the audience to rededicate their lives. Then he wanted those that had made a decision to stand up, at which point the guy in front of me stood up. This is when God decided to drive the point home. The speaker now called for those around each of those individuals to lay their hands on them and pray for them. "Oh no! Not me! Please let someone else pray for this guy! Come on, don't you know I have been heaping hot coals of indignation and judgment on this guy for the past hour and there is no way I should be praying with this guy. Come on, somebody hurry up and pray for this guy." Nobody. "Oh my gosh, you gotta be kidding me. Looks like I have to pray for this guy? This guy is going to get ripped off now, because there is no way that anything I pray is going to matter for him." I was the worst guy in the world to have pray with him, but that is how God works. Oh, and He was still not done yet either...

Fast forward to our anniversary a little while later on a neighbor island and wouldn't you know it, we ended up dining in the restaurant owned by our newly rededicated chef. And he served us free dessert. Not sure how that dessert really tasted, but I think it is about as close to the taste of a hat as you can get.

I offer up three scripture passages that are close to home for me and help me as I battle my pride day in and day out:

Romans 14:13
Therefore let us not judge one another anymore, but rather resolve this, not to put a stumbling block or a cause to fall in our brother's way.

Galatians 5:26
Let us not become conceited, provoking one another, envying one another.

Philippians 2:3,4
Let nothing be done through selfish ambition or conceit, but in lowliness of mind let each esteem others better than himself. Let each of you look out not only for his own interests, but also for the interests of others.

OVERINDULGING/EXCESS

OVERINDULGING CAN REAR its ugly head in a myriad of ways and in varying speeds. Drug addiction, alcoholism, food addiction, workaholism, and gaming addictions are only a few of the problems in this category of lures.

Drug addiction typically starts out in the formative years, when teens are experimenting with independence and peer pressure. I have been in the pond (smoke filled party houses) with my fish buddies and the water thick with lures being cast from every direction. I have watched them bite on pot, or some other "harmless" drug, and then "upgrade" to bigger lures along the way and some of them have even died in the process.

Alcoholism follows a similar profile, but in my personal experience, this has been more prevalent with my older fish buddies. I have never been tempted by the lure of drugs, but I have had my bad experiences with overindulging in alcohol. My wife has done an assessment on her personality and has determined that she has a compulsive family history and a compulsive

possibility in this area. Therefore, she chooses not to even swim in the water where that lure could be lurking and has only tasted wine once in her life. Very wise decision on her part, in my estimation, but I would not hazard to expect that behavior from anyone else, depending on his or her own personality and individual circumstances.

I have a friend who cannot stop eating. He is super sensitive and perceptive of the world around him and even enjoys writing like myself. He is very protective of his young, which is very ironic, in that his eating actually puts his relationship with his child at risk. Not a "type A" personality, stays at home most of the time, but will travel into the deep water on occasion. A definite Catfish, if you ask me. I would never dream to know how to train my friend to swim away from food, and I would never try without being asked, but it has to happen if he wants to fulfill what God has intended for him to accomplish in his child's life. It breaks my heart to know that I will one day hear that he has been pulled out of his pond from not being able to resist the lure.

Above: Moana Kali, or Blue Goatfish, are some of the tastiest and most sought after fish on the reef. They can be seen following Tevally quite often looking for leftovers.

Facing Page: It's all about the trophy shots.

Above: Aria showing off Daddy's Omilu.
A great way to bond with your little girl!

I had a boss one time that absolutely drove me crazy. He was a true workaholic. In fact, there were times that he would sleep in his office because he did not have time to go home and accomplish the tasks at hand. Of course, I thought he made the tasks at hand way more difficult than they needed to be. Then again, he was a Colonel and I never went past Major. He was, however, on his third wife and I have not gone past my first one (so far!). He wanted to be a General and was willing to sacrifice just about anything to get there. He was a big fish in a big pond and when the bait was around, he would shine like a Marlin. I hope he got what he was looking for and was happy when he got there.

The last area I will discuss here is gaming, both on-line and in person. On-line gaming is a huge industry and growing at an astonishing pace. Because of my competitive nature, I am prone to the lure of beating someone at just about anything and I have to recognize the lure and swim away. I have resisted the urge to buy a smart phone, partly because of my penchant for competition. There are so many opportunities on a smart phone for me to get caught up in everything from

angry birds to happy word games. In person gaming, or gambling, can be addictive as well. I have seen a man gamble away his life savings and lose a marriage of almost 40 years. That was one of the fisherman's biggest catches, because that fish was a pastor, a leader among men, and never recovered his ministry. The fisherman religiously used the catch and release program to set him up for huge failure later. The program was in full effect throughout his life, the lures continued to grow bigger and bigger, and he never got help along the way.

I only highlight a few of the overindulging areas because they are so vast, but I hope you see the danger in just these few examples and can find what your possible overindulgence is. Please, take an honest look at your life, what you do from day to day, and see if you can recognize any areas of overindulgence. I am not saying everyone has one, but I am willing to bet an overindulgence of money, that if you can't see a problem that truly exists, there is someone close by you that can. They simply might not be willing to let you know for some reason. If you are honestly looking, you will see it, or it will be revealed to you (probably by someone who loves you!). We, as big strong men, think we can overcome it on our own, or it does not affect anyone else around us. Look at it from a different angle though. Instead, think how it is keeping you from fulfilling everything that God has designed for you. Then you may see how the Fisherman meets his goal merely by keeping you distracted.

Proverbs 23:21
For the drunkard and the glutton will come to poverty, and slumber will clothe them with rags.

Philippians 3:19
Whose end is destruction, whose God is their belly, and whose glory is in their shame, who mind earthly things.

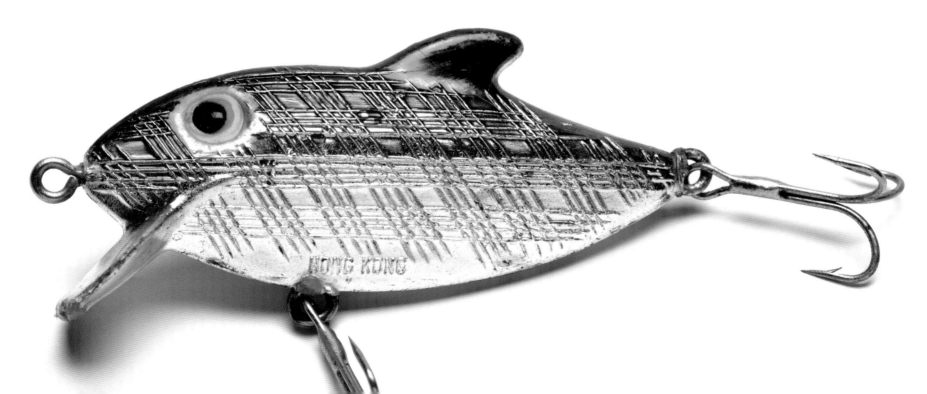

SEX/LUST

THERE IS A GIANT TRAWLER out at sea. It is sailing today with large crews, deploying and hauling in massive nets, bursting at the seams with unsuspecting bounty, at the direction of its single-minded captain. It is called the S. S. Porn. There is no effective government regulatory agency checking its haul. They do not care. There is nothing stopping the rampage and absolute decimation of our population. The porn industry is a multi-billion dollar industry. They make almost 3-times the amount of movies as Hollywood does every year and it is the fastest growing industry in the U.S. You and your children are the target and the tide is not turning. My family is a prime example of the battle being waged out there.

The first couple of years of high school dramatically changed my oldest son's life. He was very talented with computers and began to repair them for customers of the high school computer class. It was through that class that he was exposed to pornography stored on the computer hard drives. That exposure turned quickly from curiosity into a pursuit, from pursuit to obsession, and finally from obsession to addiction. By the time college started, the addiction was in full force and controlled almost all aspects of his life. He managed to finish a couple semesters, but there was no purpose and he hated himself and hated me. Life at home took continual turns for the worse (See the Anger/Aggression lure to follow) until we finally asked him to move out of our home.

Once he was out from under our supervision, he was free to do whatever he wanted and he spiraled deeper and deeper into the dark abyss of evil. We thank God continually that he finally recognized that he could not break the addiction on his own and dropped to his knees. He was miraculously delivered, hired as an intern at a church, found a full time job, and has since married a wonderful young lady. Although it is a wonderful story of divine healing, the story is not yet fully written. The Fisherman will continue to throw the lure and it would be foolish to think the battle is already won.

I reprint my oldest son's testimony in the appendix (I have removed names and made minor corrections). If

Above: It is hard to beat the peace one can feel while fishing during a sunset in Hawaii.

Facing Page: Gerry Freeman doing some arm curls with a little sturgeon.

you feel like reading it, try to pick out the lures, the ways they were cast, how they grew, and the catch and release program.

I want to stress, that dropping to your knees and asking the Lord for help could also miraculously deliver you. But, experience says maybe you will need additional help. There were no fish buddies encouraging him in any way, because he did not let anyone know about his addiction to the lure. He could not overcome the shame and self-loathing. I am asking you to try and overcome that obstacle. Although you could drop to your knees and be miraculously healed as well, maybe your path is through men sharpening each other as iron sharpens iron. You could also require deep authentic counseling and I encourage you to seek it out aggressively. It could save your life.

In my day, the Sears catalog underwear section brought about little boy giggles. Now the Victoria's Secret catalog has passed just about anything I saw as a kid. Everywhere you turn, pornography is calling for us to get entangled. It is up to all of us, including our families and our church brothers, to hold each other accountable. We have to be willing to lift each other out of the quicksand of porn. Until you can break the silence and admit to another brother that you have an issue, and need some help, you are probably going to continue to drown in the whirlpool, sucking you down. You have got to find someone you can confide in, and trust, to lock arms and avoid the lure. Your life is at stake, contrary to what the Fisherman would like you to think.

James 1:14-15

But each one is tempted when he is drawn away by his own desires and enticed. Then, when desire has conceived, it gives birth to sin; and sin, when it is full-grown, brings forth death.

Facing Page: Always looking for a little serenity out on the ocean.

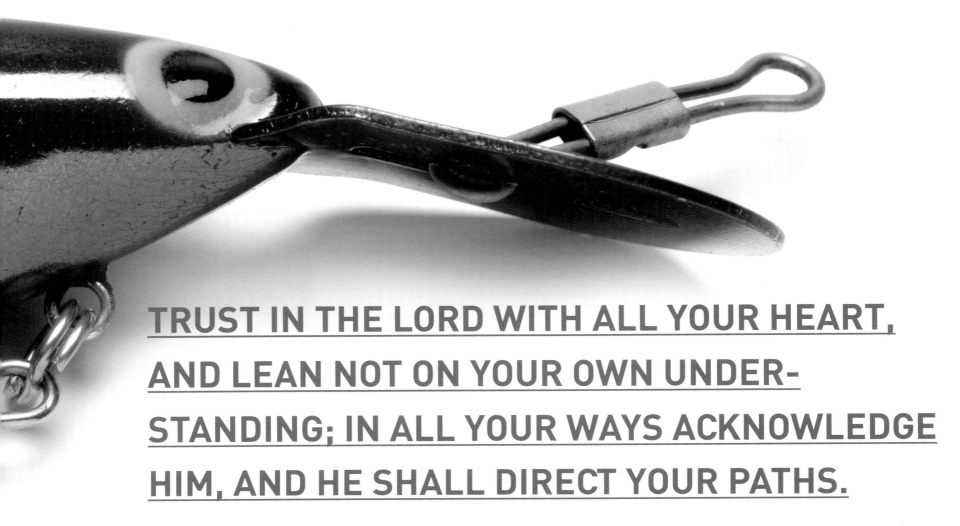

TRUST IN THE LORD WITH ALL YOUR HEART, AND LEAN NOT ON YOUR OWN UNDER-STANDING; IN ALL YOUR WAYS ACKNOWLEDGE HIM, AND HE SHALL DIRECT YOUR PATHS.

Proverbs 3:5,6

ANGER/AGGRESSION

"If you want people to go deep, you have to go first."

"If you are not going to go deep, then don't bother to write a self-help book."

"Don't get mad at me, I'm just saying...you need to go deeper."

ALL OF THIS 'DEEPER' feedback from different people was starting to get irritating. Dare I say it was making me angry. Not to mention the feedback that I was not getting. That had me more concerned. If all of these trusted sources were telling me the same thing, then I guess I really did need to examine the issue. And the way in which my wife mimicked me about my pride confession told me there were other glaring deficiencies in this book.

I woke up the next morning determined to be open about going deeper. The Lord immediately showed me two anger outbursts and more started to pop up throughout the day. I chuckled periodically as I recalled

more and more anger scenes throughout our marriage. Not because they were funny, but because it was now evident that God was revealing a pattern.

I was raised under the strict discipline of a military home. I loved it just fine and that is how I raised my own kids after I went into the military myself. Because I flew fighters, the military fostered an aggressive personality in me. They had to because they knew that hesitation could kill you as fast as anything in that environment. I remember one of my instructors pleading with me "You better learn to be more aggressive!" which directly led to me meeting and eventually marrying my wife, but that is a story for another book.

I recalled our five-year anniversary. We were all dressed up to enjoy a nice dinner somewhere, but we had to drive our toddler, Mykal, over to the grandparent's house and drop him off. As I was pulling up to exit our subdivision, a speeding car barely squeezed between me and the car in front of us. My wife immediately said, "Just let him be, it's our anniversary." I knew she was right so I determined to let it go and enjoy our evening.

Above: You only have to reach your thumb into an Uku's mouth once to figure out how sharp their teeth are.

But as I approached the next stop sign, I saw the jerk that almost killed us a couple minutes prior. That big giant lure of anger was now right in front of me. And I lunged out and bit that lure with everything in me. I looked left and right, saw that no traffic was approaching and crushed my Z-28's accelerator to the floor. I blew straight through that stop sign and passed the punk and his sidekick girlfriend. I yanked the wheel in front of him and then slammed on my brakes. I am sure my wife was yelling something by now, but I can't recall what it was as I threw open my door and exited. I could see the offender through his windshield as he put his car in reverse and started peeling out backwards to escape. I then started picking up anything I could grab on the side of the road and started throwing it at his car. He pulled away quickly and I was left standing there, huffing and puffing in a cloud of dust. I turned and walked back to my car, the evening now ruined for my beautiful bride.

I cannot tell you how many road-rages my wife has endured in our marriage (and one head-jarring introduction to my weakness even before we were

married). I think the last one was after picking up that before-mentioned toddler in high school and I managed to get into a verbal "discussion" with a carload of thugs that Mykal and my wife would rather have avoided. As I went for my seatbelt to rumble in the street, my wife leaned across my lap and said, "If you get out of the car, you are walking home!" In the past, that would not have stopped me, but I had matured a fraction in the last 15 years. And those were just the in-car incidents.

The other anger outburst that the Lord reminded me of that morning was an argument about finances (See Tarzan addiction in the Money/Toys chapter). It was the first day of a new class and I had to get to work. I did not have time to get into a long, drawn out "conversation". And once my volume started to rise, she did her natural thing and started to shut down. I hate it when she does that! To make a long story short (I know, too late), I kicked the dresser with my nice shiny black military shoes (and that dresser still has a black reminder patch on it), which really hurt my foot. Because of the pain in my foot, I then Karate-chopped the doorframe of our bathroom. The dresser may have moved a little, but I

can tell you, the doorframe did not budge a millimeter. Although I did not break anything, my hand hurt for the next six months and my foot ached for the next six years.

The last, but probably the worst, outbreak I will mention here is when Mykal was in college. (Yes, I am seeing a theme here). Mykal and I were sitting on the couch working on my real estate website and I did not notice the enemy on the bank casting a nice, big, fat anger lure right through the middle of our living room. My wife, or referee, was back on the mainland and tension was sky-high. The phone rang, Mykal answered it, and then hung it up. Or so he thought.

Within a few seconds, the phone started to make that "I am not hung up correctly" sound. I subsequently told Mykal that he did not hang up the phone properly.

"Yes, I did."

"If you had hung up the phone properly, it would not be making the sound that it is making."

"I can't help what sound the phone is making."

"Are you ever wrong? Do you ever do anything wrong?"

I do not remember what Mykal said back to me. I do, however, remember taking my fist and punching him

in the left temple and delivering a couple more shots elsewhere. Mykal quickly stood up, grabbed a large cutting board, and smashed his laptop computer with it. I then tackled Mykal on the couch, cocked my arm and screamed, "I will take you out!" several times. He cowered in fear.

We did soon apologize to each other, but life drastically changed for my family on that night. Even though I finally recognized a life stained with splashes of anger, and I determined to squash the impulses, my wife no longer felt comfortable leaving the two of us in the same house together. She could actually now drive along with me in the car, stare out the window, and say nothing. Nothing at all. We all went to counseling and the counselor told me that if something did not change soon, my wife would go into a clinical depression. My youngest boy was super sad about the whole situation and Mykal was destined to have to leave our home.

I must encourage all of you men to find a good counselor and go. I don't care if you think you don't have any issues at all. I have found that only good can come of it.

You will either work on some issues you genuinely have, you will work on issues you did not know you had, or you will prevent issues from ever arising. All good. Years later, I am happy to write, I believe my anger issues are slightly behind me, my son has left his old issues behind him, and my wife is now a counselor herself. I want to stress again to you men out there, learn what the anger and aggression lures look like in your life, see when they are being cast in front of you, and do what it takes to turn away.

I offer below a few scripture references that are helpful to me. I trust that they will steer you in the right direction to seeing and avoiding the lure of anger.

Proverbs 14:29
Whoever is slow to anger has great understanding, but he who has a hasty temper exalts folly.

Proverbs 19:11
Good sense makes one slow to anger, and it is his glory to overlook an offense.

Galatians 5:19-21

Now the works of the flesh are evident: sexual immorality, impurity, sensuality, idolatry, sorcery, enmity, strife, jealousy, fits of anger, rivalries, dissensions, divisions, envy, drunkenness, orgies, and things like these. I warn you, as I warned you before, that those who do such things will not inherit the kingdom of God.

Colossians 3:8, 12-13

But now you must put them all away: anger, wrath, malice, slander, and obscene talk from your mouth. Put on then, as God's chosen ones, holy and beloved, compassionate hearts, kindness, humility, meekness, and patience, bearing with one another and, if one has a complaint against another, forgiving each other; as the Lord has forgiven you, so you also must forgive.

Ephesians 4:26-28

Be angry and do not sin; do not let the sun go down on your anger, and give no opportunity to the devil. Let the thief no longer steal, but rather let him labor, doing honest work with his own hands, so that he may have something to share with anyone in need.

Matthew 5:21-24

"You have heard that it was said to those of old, 'You shall not murder; and whoever murders will be liable to judgment.' But I say to you that everyone who is angry with his brother will be liable to judgment; whoever insults his brother will be liable to the council; and whoever says, 'You fool!' will be liable to the hell of fire. So if you are offering your gift at the altar and there remember that your brother has something against you, leave your gift there before the altar and go. First be reconciled to your brother, and then come and offer your gift..."

MONEY/TOYS

WHEN I WAS A YOUNG teenager, my grandfather gave me two books: Tarzan the Terrible and Tarzan the Untamed. They were a two-volume jungle tale on what happened when the Nazis burned Tarzan's home down and took Jane captive during World War II. I still love the story and at the time it spoke to my spirit of adventure. I would imagine living in the wild and fending for myself and hunting big game.

One day, I happened into an antique store in southern Georgia and came upon a shelf of more Tarzan books and some glossy movie black and whites of Johnny Weissmuller and Maureen O'Sullivan. I bought it all and my collecting bug grew with a vengeance. I soon moved to California and a fellow collector introduced me to another level of acquiring the memorabilia. Every three months I would go to the world-renowned San Mateo Toy Fair and I was constantly combing the surrounding cities looking for more books and toys. It became an obsession. My license plate was TRZN NUT. When we moved to Alabama, I had my own room in the house

and I got a second business outside the military to fund my purchasing habit. We argued over how much I spent and you might think this sounds funny, but there came a time when my wife sat on my lap and we discussed me going to counseling. For collecting Tarzan stuff.

One time, I tried to prove to myself that I was not a Tarzan addict. I decided, in order to prove it, that I would sell my most prized possession in the collection. It was a full set of 1933 gum cards called Tarzan and the Crystal Vaults of Isis. I had purchased them for $750 from someone in Los Angeles and I loved to look at those cards. Anyway, I mustered my strength, called another collector from Denver and sold them for $2000. Victory!

Facing Page: It can be a lot of fun to go to a fish auction and see all the different kinds of fish available.

I was not an addict! Shortly thereafter, I purchased the French version and an English version for $5700 spending the money we had saved for a second car.

The point in that story is to show how collecting can turn into hoarding and enthusiasm can turn into an obsession. For just about anything in your life. And, I really think some of it can be genetic. My great aunt was a world-class doll collector and had them all throughout her huge house. My grandfather had his own room, stacked from the floor to the ceiling with guns. And my father spent every extra penny on coins for a part of his life. Even researching this book, I had to resist the urge to collect old fishing lures!

I know this can also spill over into the Overindulging category, but you need to ask yourself if there are any unhealthy areas, or levels, of focus in your life. Is your sports enthusiasm at a healthy level? TV? Gaming? Are you constantly looking for a better car? House? Clothes? What gets in between you and your relationship with God? Don't get in a position where you want to do more for the kingdom of God, but you get caught in the

conundrum of having to choose. I offer the following story as an example:

Matthew 19:16-22

Now behold, one came and said to Him, "Good Teacher, what good thing shall I do that I may have eternal life?" So He said to him, "Why do you call Me good? No one is good but One, that is, God. But if you want to enter into life, keep the commandments." He said to Him, "Which ones?" Jesus said, "'You shall not murder,' 'You shall not commit adultery,' 'You shall not steal,' 'You shall not bear false witness,' The young man said to Him, "All these things I have kept from my youth. What do I still lack?" Jesus said to him, "If you want to be perfect, go, sell what you have and give to the poor, and you will have treasure in heaven; and come, follow Me." But when the young man heard that saying, he went away sorrowful, for he had great possessions.

I don't believe God will necessarily ask you to go and sell everything you own, but He will highlight if those things represent a barrier in your spiritual life.

HOW DOES THE ENEMY CHOOSE THE RIGHT LURE FOR US?

AS I STATED BEFORE, it comes down to what type of fish personality you have. If you are a Bluegill, and you are not attracted to the Bomber that just came thrashing by, you can't pat yourself on the back and be proud you did not bite. It was not meant for you. It was meant for that Bass you know, lurking in the lilies nearby. You might even want that Bass to bite. Then he would not be around to bother you and your little world. You, however, need to be worried about the little bobber that plunks in front of you with a teeny, tiny piece of bread on a teeny, tiny hook hanging below. For some reason, you find that very attractive and your Bass buddy won't even give it a second look. If only the two of you cared about each other. If only the two of you could collaborate and warn each other that those lures are not authentic, that they are fakes, and that the Fisherman is standing on the bank, casting away.

The point I am making here is to avoid being proud of the fact you resisted the lure designed for someone else. You should be no more proud of that than being proud you are not a Bass. You are called to be the best Bluegill

you can be, the one you were designed to be. In order to accomplish that goal, however, you need to focus on your own lures, instead of avoiding those of others.

I can no more be proud that I resisted the Calloway clubs, than I can be proud of the fact that I have Hazel eyes. I do look good with my Hazel eyes (just kidding), but I need to work on my pride issues (can't you tell?). Only then can I become the best Wahoo that I can be, and was designed to be, and that has a great and mighty Wahoo purpose and future. I hope and pray that I sense the dangerous waters and turn away. I hope and pray I find my best future and follow the steps toward it. That will only happen with the leading of the Lord and the help of my brothers.

SECTION TWO / CONCLUSIONS

A S I OUTLINED, the Fisherman is on the shores of your life, casting lures to hook you. He is fiercely and passionately focused on catching you, destroying you, and ruining the plan that God has set before you. He knows you inside and out. He knows your strengths and he knows your weaknesses, probably better than you do. So when he opens his tackle box and surveys what he has available, he will find a lure that you like. He will pull it out of the tray and smile. He will carefully tie his line, step near your world, and deftly pull that lure into your life. If you are not prepared, you will bite.

The list of lures that we examined is by no means all-inclusive, but I believe it is indicative of what is available to the Fisherman to hook men. Good, strong and upstanding men. Pillars of society. Role models to those around them. And the more visible to a cynical population, the better for the Fisherman. Don't let him do it. Don't let him succeed in your life. Don't let him divert you from accomplishing what God has called you to fulfill in life. Be ready for the lure. With divine clarity, recognize it and boldly exercise a strategy that you planned before the lure even entered your waters.

Section III details a plan for protecting your life. It is a simple plan, but takes a purposeful resolve on your part for it to work. Don't be afraid! Grab all that God has for you and achieve everything that you are capable of with His divine help. I invite you to keep this brilliant quote from Francis Chan in mind as you do, though:

"Our greatest fear should not be of failure but of succeeding at things in life that don't really matter." Francis Chan

Now let's move forward and look at five steps that can help you do just that...

Above: Kimi Werner proving once again that she is one with the ocean.

Facing Page: Once the poles are in the water, the big stories start to get told on the beach.

How do I resist the fisherman's lures?

NO

UNATTENDED VEHICLES
UNATTENDED VESSELS
DRINKING OF
INTOXICATING LIQUOR
LITTERING

SUZUKI

BE AWARE, THERE IS A FISHERMAN OUT TO CATCH YOU

I may think I am swimming along just fine, minding my own business, and the ocean (or lake, or stream) is too big for me to worry about a so-called Fisherman. I could not be further from the truth. I must take a step back and look at my life from the outside. If the Fisherman is not assailing me, maybe I am not doing much for the Kingdom right now. Maybe the Fisherman is not focused on me quite yet, but he will be some day. Especially if I find out what God wants me to do with my life. For now, he may be content to let me grow bigger and bigger, right where I am, and come back for me later.

Wouldn't it be funny if there really were a "school" for fish? Imagine the trout gathering together in a deep eddy, around their wet-erase board. They would map out how each of their friends got yanked out of the river. How Old Fred saw a big, fat fly go floating by that looked too good to be true. Even though it rested

a little too low in the water, and the season for those flies was well past, he bit on it anyway. They saw him fight for his life, but it was too late. The next thing anyone knew, Fred was gone. And how Henry was warned not to go after anything when the dark shadow was near the bank. He threw caution to the wind and ignored the warnings. Henry is now gone, too. Maybe these fish in fish school would start working as a team, helping each other avoid those fake flies. Maybe they would start telling each other when danger seemed to be nearby. But, they don't. They would probably keep to themselves and live their lives trying to overcome the problems on their own. Just like we do.

Above: The big ones that did not get away.

Facing Page: I don't believe you can bond any closer with your children than while fishing with them.

Unfortunately, many church services are reduced to self-help clinics. There are plenty of talks on how I can feel better about myself, or how we can all just get along. It is a tragedy that we can forget there is a nasty enemy, roaming the banks, wholly focused on our destruction. He is out to destroy our future, our marriages, and our ability to effectively use our lives as a witness. He may not be able to land us, but if he can make our lives irrelevant to those around us, he does not need to even get us on the line.

We, as men, need to get together and talk frankly, and factually, about the Fisherman. He is real and he has many helpers. We need to understand his destructive mentality and his evil desires. We also need to talk about our weaknesses among ourselves, so that we can strengthen each other, as Paul said:

2 Corinthians 12:9
And He said to me, "My grace is sufficient for you, for My strength is made perfect in weakness." Therefore most gladly I will rather boast in my infirmities, that the power of Christ may rest upon me.

Above: If we could only see how many lines the enemy has out to catch us on a daily basis, it might look like this.

BE AWARE, THE FISHERMAN USES LURES THAT YOU LIKE

When the fisherman from Oregon steps down to the bank and readies his fishing pole for a Steelhead, he does not pull out a 5½ ounce Marlin Magic lure. He, more likely, will pull out a Wicked Spinner to entice it instead. Correspondingly, when a new set of Callaway Golf Clubs is tossed in front of me, I am not interested. It is not going to work. There was a time in my life when I would have liked a set, to show off on the links, or let people guess at my handicap, but I don't golf anymore and it has lost its shiny allure. I am, however, not so confident that other lures will not work on me.

I need to be vigilant to find out what those lures are and build my defenses. I know I have an ego, I am very competitive, and I like to win. I like to be better than others, so I am tempted to point out other people's flaws. I can be prideful, and that is wrong. That lure is thrown in front of me day in and day out. How do I know about that lure? From scripture and my little "Cleaner Fish".

Did I ever learn that from any men in my life? Probably not. But, I think we can come together and resolve to help each other out if we each care. And I hope I am getting better and better at recognizing my lures and let them float on by.

What is your lure? When you read the scripture, is there anything that jumps out from time to time and you say, "That's me"? Is it things or possessions? Is it security? Is it comfort? Is it pride? Is it lust? Do you covet anything? Are you jealous? If you ask the Lord to reveal to you what your lures are, he will reveal them through the Word, through your "Cleaner Fish" and friends, or to your mind. But, you have to really want to know and really want to resist.

I have a fish buddy that comes to me and laments, from time to time, that he knows he is doing wrong. He knows he is hurting his wife and will eventually hurt his son, when he finds out how he hurt her mom. He knows that there is impending doom to his marriage down the road, but he bites on the lures, time and time again. His drive to save all of that does not outweigh the biting of the lures. And it drives him crazy. But, until he drops to his knees, surrenders, and truly asks for the help he needs from the only one that can provide it, he will ultimately fail. He does not know the marvelous plans that God has intended for his life and he does not know that the Fisherman is the one casting the lures.

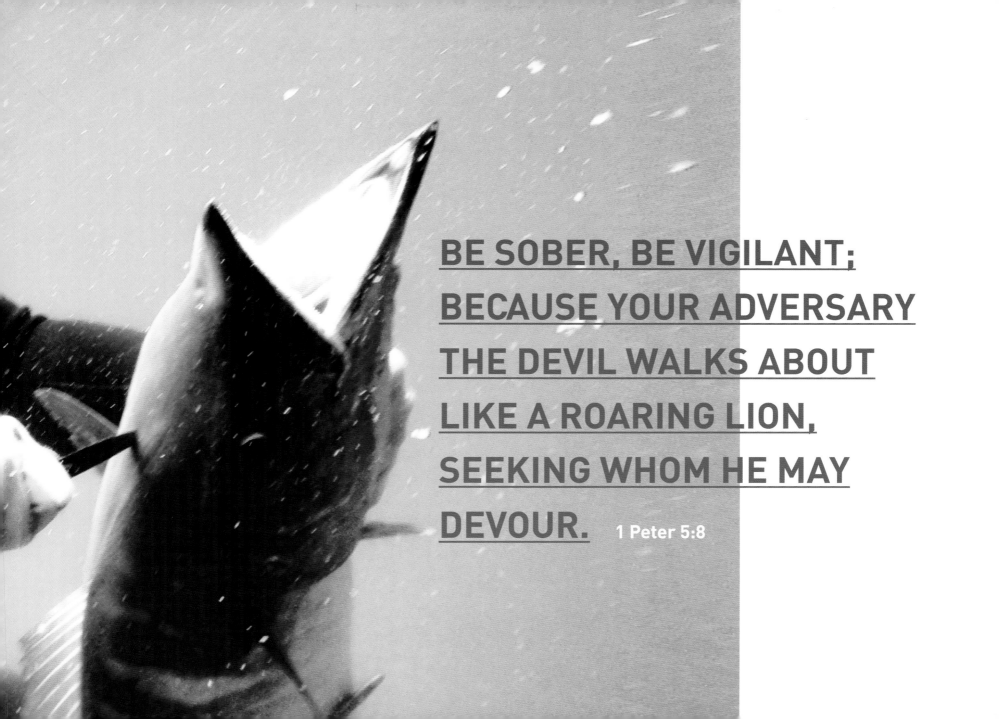

BE SOBER, BE VIGILANT; BECAUSE YOUR ADVERSARY THE DEVIL WALKS ABOUT LIKE A ROARING LION, SEEKING WHOM HE MAY DEVOUR. 1 Peter 5:8

RECOGNIZE AUTHENTICITY

I am sure that most people have heard by now, how federal agents recognize counterfeit money. They do not study counterfeit bills. Instead, they study authentic bills so in depth, they will always be able to tell when they see a fake. Men need to study authentic spirituality, authentic relationships, authentic marriages, authentic work environments, and authentic financial goals so in depth that they will immediately recognize a fake when it is tossed in front of them.

Authentic spirituality genuinely seeks to find the God of the universe and have a relationship with Him. Authentic spirituality follows the guidelines outlined in the Bible that fosters finding that God. Authentic spirituality dutifully looks in those Holy pages for those guidelines. Authentic spirituality seeks to burn away the dross of sin that clouds that search. Authentic spirituality puts a life under the microscope to genuinely find that sin so that it can be burned away. Authentic spirituality partners with other Christians

seeking authentic spirituality. Authentic spirituality severs partnerships with those that hamper that goal. Authentic spirituality builds authentic relationships.

Authentic relationships seek to reveal truth. Authentic relationships hide as little as possible. Authentic relationships look to build the other partner to their highest levels. Authentic relationships acknowledge failures. Authentic relationships seek for humility and burn away pride. Authentic relationships seek forgiveness. Authentic relationships honor the other partner as God intended. Authentic relationships sometimes lead to authentic marriages.

Above: Funny, I remember this shot a little different on that day.

Facing Page: Alexandra Fly based on Bates' pattern in Streamer Fly Tying and Fishing (1950) Wikimedia Commons

131

Above: Randy Kimura posing on Facebook (with MY fish!)

Authentic marriages treasure the institution of marriage. Authentic marriages build fortresses around their relationships. Authentic marriages are very, very hard. Authentic marriages take lots and lots of work. Authentic marriages are worth that work. Authentic marriages get counseling, whether it is needed or not. Authentic marriages put God as the head of the household. Authentic marriages build authentic work situations.

Authentic work situations have authentic goals. Authentic work situations foster healthy, productive environments. Authentic work situations have great employees and bosses. Authentic work situations lead to authentic financial goals.

Authentic financial goals acknowledge that God has made it all and owns it all. Authentic financial goals give honor to the provider of the finances. Authentic financial goals have solid, achievable steps. Authentic financial goals follow biblical guidelines and are probably built with godly advisors.

The bottom line here is that authenticity prevents many, many foolish mistakes. What lure is taunting you and begging you to study authenticity?

RECOGNIZE FAKES

Although I may be getting better at recognizing authenticity, it is probably still a good idea for me to learn to recognize fakes. What does a fake look like? Well, first of all, it looks like what is cautioned about in the Bible. It looks like a consoling, friendly lady when you and your wife have just had a fight. It possibly looks like a drink with the boys again, when the family is at home eating together. It says, "You wouldn't buy a pair of shoes before trying them on, would you?" It might look like a job opportunity and all you have to do is tell a little white lie or stab a coworker in the back. It may even look like a football game on Sunday, if I never spend time alone with God. By the way, I am not against football, per se. I just think that a priority should be set to spend as much time rooting for my relationship with Jesus as I root for my favorite sports team. And I am figuratively looking in the mirror when I say that.

Fakes are presented to us all day long. We can get up in the morning and look in the mirror and figure we need fake hair to promote our fake selves. We can hop into our shiny cars that promote our fake financial situations on our way to our jobs that we fake that we like. We can fake who we are all day, so we can be what other people want us to be, so we can get the fake gold pocket watch in the end.

God has a real plan for the real you. It is a beautiful story with a fabulous ending. You are the main character, and you don't have to act. You can be you. And you can be real.

WHEN IN DOUBT - SWIM AWAY!

Let's travel all the way back to section I to my story of spearfishing Ono with Jonah. In that scenario, the Ono that has the highest survivability rate, is the one that encounters us on the outskirts, has a bad feeling, and leaves right away. Even the one that decides to swim through the area and exit to the other side, may get a miracle spear shot in the side from one of us. It is better

not to risk it and make a decision to swim away. I am reminded of one encounter in my younger days.

Between my sophomore and junior year of college, I travelled to Abilene, Texas, to study some of the military organizations at Dyess Air Force Base. At least that was during the day. There was almost nothing to do at night in Abilene in 1981, except to go to Graham Central Station. It was an enormous bar/dance club with two dance floors and you could not even see from one end of it to the other. A bunch of my newly made friends and I decided to head over as we heard it was the only place to go.

I remember leaning against the bar, watching the huge group of dancers slowly circle the dance floor, as the music played. After a while, I noticed there was one particular lady, dancing with another man, repeatedly looking at me throughout the night. I told some of my friends and they responded that I was imagining things. They eventually confirmed what I was seeing and they told me to "go for it". I had no intention of doing that, so I remained at my post and continued to mind my

Above: Pink-Winged Flying Fish escaping danger" Credit NOAA images.

own business. For a while, anyway. My heart started pounding in fear when I saw the lady in question start walking towards me across the dance floor. She came over, grabbed my hand and drug me out into the crowd and we started to dance, or that was what I called it. My roommate told me, later that evening, it looked more like two animals mating. After working up a sweat, the music finally stopped temporarily, and she went to "freshen up" and wanted to go someplace else with me. Thankfully, when she went into the bathroom, I ran into the parking lot and convinced someone to drive me away. I don't know what would have happened if I would have stuck around, but quite possibly something I would regret.

First of all, there are innumerable problems with the situation I put myself into. Being at that dance club was a bit like being a Herring on opening fishing day in Sitka, Alaska. I put myself in a precarious position to be netted by countless Fishermen and I was lucky to dodge the bullet. I probably should not have been there in the first place, looked at her longer than I did, or went dancing with her. Thankfully, I was naïve and

scared and chose to run like Joseph did from Potiphar's wife. I found out later, when I coincidentally came across her desk at the civil engineering office, that she was married and was not dancing with her husband that evening. Days later, I even saw her with another man eating lunch, we talked briefly, and I turned and ran again. She was the lure for many men. And a lot of them were biting and ruining their lives and the lives of those around them.

Facing Page: The little red Menpachi have big eyes to see when they come out at night from their holes in the reef. Tasty little buggahs…

At this point in the book, you should have a little bit of an idea what the lures are that you might be susceptible to. You should be able to mentally open the Fisherman's Tackle Box and find the tray that is marked especially for you. If you are like me, there are several different trays, each having a special section just for my unique and particular weaknesses. You should start to work on recognizing when those lures are cast in front of you. You should also work on having a set strategy for exiting or avoiding the situation.

We have not really looked at how to exit the lure-infested area. There is a lot of peer pressure and so many different situations, so we each should have more than one strategy to get out of those dangerous waters. I think we can boil it all down to four firewalls: **Run, Read, Relate, and Refurbish.**

RUN I think the first and most effective method is to run. Literally. I gave you an example where I ran away from a huge lure that was thrown in front of me. When you run, you can at least get out of the area and possibly think more clearly. When my son is presented with the lure of porn, he is most effective when he literally gets up from the computer, or wherever he is, and runs. He goes for a jog to burn off the energy and gives himself the opportunity to think and pray. People that are being tempted with food, drugs, gaming, or other lures have maintained effective distance by running. If you physically can't run away, then run away mentally. Think about something else. Think about healthy things. Recite scripture in your head, or better yet, out loud. Build a place you can go to in your mind for protection. Think of your future and the great plans ahead.

READ The Lord can very effectively speak to you through His word. A mighty mental and spiritual fortress will be built by spending time in the Bible. Every weapon available at your disposal is found there. Every hope and dream in your life is found there. Every bit of the love for you from God is outlined there. Every scheme of the enemy is found there. If you don't go there and read, think of all that you will miss out on. Besides the Bible, there are other wonderful wellsprings of wisdom available for you to read. The best, of course, is The Tackle Box (Okay, I am kidding again!). Honestly, pick up some tried and true books from the great spiritual pillars of the past and present. Keep giving yourself new insights and revelations on the scriptures and how to apply them in your life. See how others have avoided the enemy and found a relationship with the Lord.

RELATE

Relate to God. Relate to the loved one in your life. Relate to the brothers in your life that seek for your prosperity and success. And relate to yourself. Find out who you really are and who you should become. I know, I know, I keep saying that over and over. I am just trying to hammer it home that God has wonderful things designed for you to be and great works for you to accomplish.

REFURBISH

The Lord can very effectively speak to you through His word. A mighty mental and spiritual fortress will be built by spending time in the Bible. Every weapon available at your disposal is found there. Every hope and dream in your life is found there. Every bit of the love for you from God is outlined there. Every scheme of the enemy is found there. If you don't go there and read, think of all that you will miss out on. Besides the Bible, there are other wonderful wellsprings of wisdom available for you to read. The best, of course, is The Tackle Box (Okay, I am kidding again!). Honestly,

pick up some tried and true books from the great spiritual pillars of the past and present. Keep giving yourself new insights and revelations on the scriptures and how to apply them in your life. See how others have avoided the enemy and found a relationship with the Lord.

Tell God that you will resolve to do better, with His help. Tell God that you want to figure out what the lures are in your life and you will determine to avoid them through the steps we have just outlined. Remind yourself that you are a child of the King and that you want to inherit all that the King has for you. Remind yourself that you, through forgiveness, are washed white as snow and can start fresh again. The power of God is always available when you repent and ask. Tell God that you will seek the help of those brothers around you and you will help them as well. It is a new day and God can give you a fresh outpouring of the Holy Spirit. In the words of the old gospel hymn, "Your future's so bright, you gotta wear shades."

Above: Hannah doing a little Catfish wrangling.

139

SECTION THREE / CONCLUSIONS

IF YOU ARE ANYTHING LIKE ME, you need simple, understandable and actionable steps that can be remembered in the critical times that you need them. And, I believe it is much easier to remember things, if you are passionate about them. Hopefully, the five steps just outlined will make you at least a little more effective in battling the Fisherman. You know he is out there, using the most attractive, you-focused lures he can find to catch you. You also know those lures are fake. Further, you know you are going to have to do a little bit of work to be able to discern the difference from the authentic goals you should be striving for. Finally, whenever you feel that a lure is possibly being cast in your direction, in some form or another, you need to run away. Don't stop to think, or do anything else, just start running.

Above: If there is a better way to catch fish, people will figure it out somehow (Wikimedia commons)

What do I do once I'm hooked?

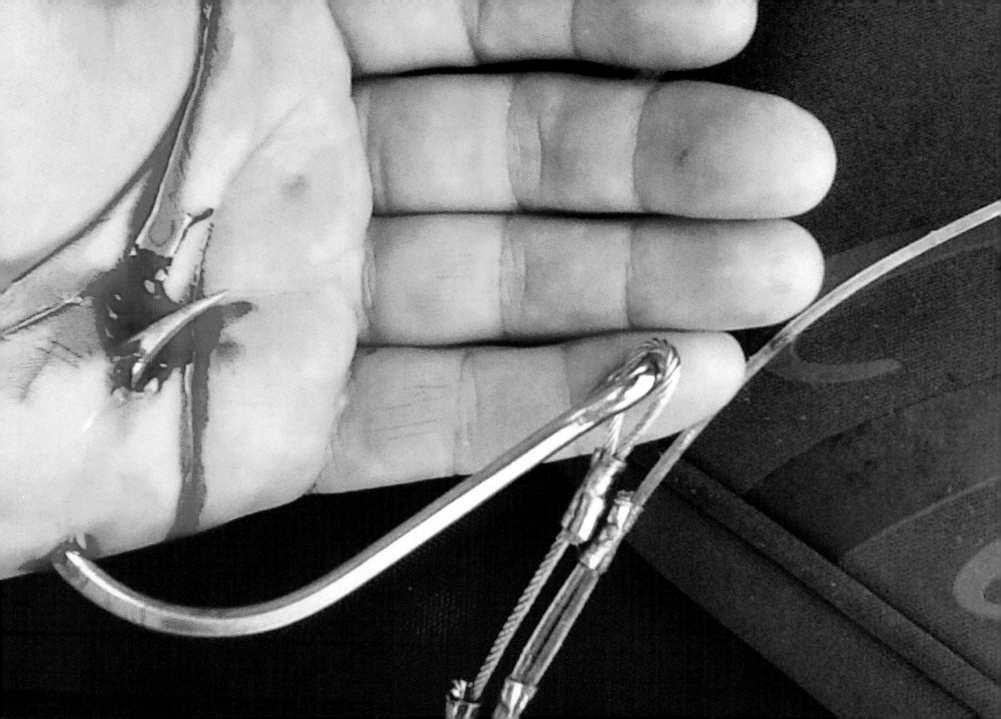

THREE ACTIONABLE STEPS TO SURVIVAL

Fish are extremely smart, or their sense of survival is so high, that they prove elusive to many fishermen. If only men were so keen on staying spiritually alive! We can, at times, go right back to where we failed and do it all over again, making it worse that it was before:

If we can immediately spit out the lure when it is detected, or violently shake the lure off at the first sign of pain, or even surrender in the battle, we might escape to live another day. Let's look at each one of these steps in a little bit more detail...

1 SPIT IT OUT!

A fish's mouth is a super sensitive area, just like ours. Much of our world is experienced through the senses in our mouth. It is the same with fish. It has to be for them to survive. They need to be able to detect if they have ingested the correct food. Fishing line companies spend millions of dollars researching and developing line that is harder and harder for fish to detect. Is it clear enough, is it strong enough for the tensile strength allotted, and is it flexible enough? Of course, fishing lure companies spend even more to make their lures as life-like as possible so that the lure is as effective as possible. By the time the fish figures it out, hopefully it is too late.

Another fascinating aspect of the fishing world is the hook itself. Hooks are almost as diverse as fish. There is a different style of hook for not only every fish species, but also designed for the different sizes of those species you have targeted, and the baits you will use. For example, the hook designed for a Giant Trevally, when using live bait, is almost round. And the tip of the hook has a very slight bend and is extremely sharp. It is designed so that when the Trevally bites onto the bait and keeps swimming, the eyelet will start exiting the mouth, but that tip will catch around the cartilage of the fish's lip. Then you want the leverage on the hook to encircle and drive the tip through the soft part of the

Above: Pastor "Sumo" Sato and his son Micah out in Fiji having a good time.

Facing Page: I learned not to let the fish go too quickly after you get the first hook out if there are two hooks in the lure.

Chapter Intro Photo: Bloody decks thanks to Tsutomu Lures.

mouth and the barb to hold it in. And every fish has a hook designed just as thoroughly for them. You have to know the Fisherman is no less thoughtful of the hooks designed for you.

The Fisherman will pick the line that has just the right strength for you. Not too strong to make it detectable, but not too weak to break. It will be almost invisible to you unless you are on your guard. And it will send signals up the line to let the Fisherman know you are playing with it. He will have picked out the right hook with the correct design for your mouth. It will be smooth and almost painless when it is set. Unless you can spit it out right away!

What does spitting it out mean to you? It means you have figured out there is a lure in your mouth. You have allowed yourself to get into the wrong environment and you have gone a little too far. You are sitting in front of the computer and you have clicked on the wrong advertisement flashing on the side. The adrenaline is being released into your blood stream. Spit it out now! Or you have taken a sip of alcohol that you said you would not have for a specific period of time. Spit it out (literally) now! Or you have just walked into the hotel room with a business partner and you have no business being there. Spit it out now! Whatever your lure is, you feel it in your mouth.

You are smarter than a fish. You know when the lure is in your mouth. You probably recognize it from being hooked before. Don't think it is too late. Don't think, "I have already failed, so I will keep eating, looking, feeling, drinking...or whatever." It is never too late to show your commitment to yourself and to God. Take the opportunity for even the smallest victory when you can. So, spit it out now!

2 SHAKE IT OFF!

Once a fish is hooked, typically the first thing they do is violently try to throw the hook. You will see the Marlin tail walking across the ocean surface, thrashing their head back and forth trying to dislodge the hook. If you flash back to my Bass story, you will remember how it jumped out of the water and threw my Jitterbug loose. Dorado, or Mahi Mahi, are also famous for summersaulting and twirling through the air trying desperately to get the lures out of their mouth.

We need to be no less violent in throwing our lures. And to aggressively throw a lure that you did not spit out,

you will probably need help. There are several sources to help you throw the lure:

Your accountability partner

Your pastor

Your spouse, depending on the situation

Your counselor

Guys are famously known for thinking they are the masters of their world. We don't need a map. We don't need directions or instructions. We like to think we can do a lot of things ourselves. We are strong and able to overcome. And the Fisherman will use that confidence and pride to accomplish what he wants. It took a lot of prayer on my wife's part for me to finally agree to go see a counselor. Pride kept getting in the way. Now, I have seen the benefits and highly recommend it to all men. It helps you to get outside perspectives and different strategies for solving the myriad problems we face every day. We don't know it all and the sooner we figure that out, the sooner we can get help.

Above: Emery Abilla showing us how to bring in the Oama.

148

3 SURRENDER

When you are charter fishing, one of the sweetest things ever screamed into the air is, "Fish on!" Trying not to slip, you will run to the deck chair, sit down, grab the rod, and the deck hand will get you connected and strapped in. As he does that, do you know what he is yelling in your ear? Things like, "Keep the rod tip up! Keep reeling! Don't let the line go slack! Make sure the line reels in evenly across the spool! Get that rod tip back up!" He may be yelling some other things as well, but this is a ministry book, so I won't print those.

The reason he is yelling all those things is so the line won't go slack. If it does, then the fish will have the opportunity to extract the hook. As long as there is pressure on the eyelet of the hook, it will probably stay wrapped around the jaw of the fish, or through the cheek. And that goes for almost any time a fish is on the line and hooked. I have seen the dejected look of the crew if you let the line go slack, or if the fish decides to quit pulling, and the fish gets loose.

Let's get back to you. If you have not managed to spit out the lure, or shake it loose, your best bet at this point is to surrender. In fact, it is best to surrender way before you get to this point. What I mean by that is to quit fighting against the enemy on your own. Quit doing what the Fisherman wants, struggling desperately all by yourself. Get the line slack by dropping to your knees. Ask God for divine help. Do you remember the example of my son and his addiction to pornography? He was not able to spit out the lure. He was not able to shake the addiction. It was only after he quit trying to fight it himself that he was miraculously delivered. He finally dropped to his knees, with great humility, and asked for the creator of the universe to intervene on his behalf. I

BLESSED IS THE MAN WHO TRUSTS IN THE LORD, AND WHOSE HOPE IS THE LORD.

Jeremiah 17:7

have heard countless testimonials of miraculous healing and deliverance by giving up the controls. It reminds me of my flying days when I was learning to recover an aircraft that has stalled. When an aircraft stalls, or loses its lift capabilities, the natural reaction is to pull on the stick in an attempt to lift the nose back up. The correct way to recover it, however, is to let go of the controls, let the aircraft gain some lift giving speed, and then you can attempt to pull out of the dive. Hopefully, you are not too close to the ground by then!

One critical thing to remember is that surrender is an action. Surrender is not just giving up and quitting the fight and letting the Fisherman reel you in. Surrender is dropping to your knees and asking God what the next action steps are. Maybe it includes confession to someone you hurt or confession to your new team of helpers. Maybe it includes building partnerships with fellow warriors. Maybe it includes another action word called forgiveness. Many think that forgiveness is only an attitude as well. It is just as much of an action as surrender. Surrender can include joining a group. Surrender can include leading a group. I am reminded

how Alcoholics Anonymous was started in 1935 by Bill Wilson and Dr. Bob Smith. They acknowledged that they could not overcome alcohol on their own and needed divine intervention. With God's help, they developed the 12-step program that has changed countless lives over the decades. Again, surrender is action – action with God at the helm.

It takes a purposeful resolve to survive when you are hooked. The enemy wants you to believe there is no hope. He wants you to eventually give up trying. But don't. You have too much to lose, too much to gain, and you have people that will pull for you, if you let them. Spit out those lures, shake off the hooks, and surrender your life to God's will. Imagine your future, untangled from the mess. Start to see your success and look for the bright plans laid out for you:

Jeremiah 29:11

For I know the thoughts that I think toward you, says the Lord, thoughts of peace and not of evil, to give you a future and a hope.

Above: Red Bull Air Racer Pete McLeod pulling in some tasty dinner.

151

SECTION FOUR / CONCLUSIONS

HAVE A FRIEND that had a great marriage to a beautiful wife with wonderful kids. His career was going very well and life was just grand. His personality, like mine, is also much like a Wahoo. He is aggressive, he runs in small packs, he is adventurous, fast living and he likes shiny things. So, the Fisherman threw a nice custom, shiny lure, quite a while ago, with his personal name on it. He was caught and released multiple times. To the point of being numb. He did not feel the need to spit out the lure any longer. And he avoided an accountability partner, his pastor, and would not seek counsel when caught. He decided to just keep pulling on the line, by himself and lie to all those around him. He defiantly did not drop to his knees, even in the face of the obvious. The Fisherman came to steal, kill and destroy. It was subtle at first, but in the end their joy was stolen, the marriage was killed, and lives were destroyed on many levels. It made me very sad to see what happened and he was part of the reason I wrote this book.

I woke up one morning and this book was laid out so clearly and miraculously on my mind. I bounced the idea off of my wife and then a mutual friend and they both encouraged me on several levels. I could not wait to start writing and they ended up creating a monster. I wrote pretty solid for days and days, thinking of all the men that had fallen to the lures of the enemy. There were too many examples that came to my mind and I wanted to help in some way. Most men absolutely refuse to pick up a self-help book. We don't need help. We just need to fix something or build something or conquer something. That "something" can't be us. We will, however, pick up a book on fishing. I hope that you learned a little bit about fishing and learned even more about not biting.

I hope that this book has been enjoyable for you to read. I had a blast writing it. More importantly, I hope that there were a few tidbits of information and strategies that can remind you of what is at stake and how to overcome in the battle. The odds are huge, but the prize is eternal. God bless and happy fishing...

Above: This Ulua had three lobster inside. I like his taste in food!

Facing Page: My Dad hoisting a nice trout and sporting a groovy hat back in the day with my cousin Carl.

153

A SON'S LETTER

All of my life I had been your average "Christian". I was born into a Christian home and my family and I have attended church every Sunday since as long as I can remember. My parents Vince & Julie Daubenspeck, thankfully, raised my sister Jacqui, my brother Carter, and I directly in line with the teachings of the Bible, as best as they knew how. At an early age I began searching for the Lord and wondering what my purpose here on this earth was. I recall asking my mother questions about God and her telling me all about Jesus and what He had done for me at the cross. I asked Jesus into my life at the age of 6 on September 16th, 1994 while my Pre-K class was praying for our lunch. I was so happy that day, I went home and told my mother what I had done. I was baptized shortly thereafter by my grandfather, who at the time was a minister. That was the beginning of my up and down relationship with The Lord.

My father served his 20 years in the Air Force to earn his retirement, meaning that we moved around a lot in my younger years. I was born in California and from there we moved to Alabama, Hawaii, Germany, and then back to Hawaii again. My life came under a lot of fire when I was in Germany. I was there from the age of 7 to 10. Along with the hardships of having to learn a new language, from my siblings and I being sent to German schools, I had to put up with little bullies who hated me, merely because I was an American. My brother and I got into fights all of the time with other boys. At times I felt that all my brother and I had was each other... It didn't matter who started it, we wouldn't leave each other's side no matter how big or old the other boys were. I feel those few years of fighting alongside one-another brought us closer together than most people can know.

Germany was the first place I remember having demonic encounters in my life. I used to lay awake at night trying to hide myself beneath my covers trying to ignore the darkness in the corners of my room. Trying to ignore those faint red eyes staring back at me, if l were to peek out from beneath them. Afraid to tell anyone because of what I thought they would think of me, I lived in that fear as long as I can remember being there. The cold chills I would get at night as if something evil was sweeping over my covers... sometimes I would burst into a sweat, eventually falling asleep from what I believe was from the mere exhaustion from all the stress and exertion of my energies because of the great fears I had lying in that cold bed at night.

Germany was also the first place I remember encountering pornographic material in one form or another. Europe's culture in general is much more lenient when it comes to nudity, whether it be at beaches or on the television. We used to be babysat by another German family in our little farm town. I remember there being just your average everyday show on TV with some model with her top off exposing herself for the entertainment of men. I absolutely despised it and used to get angry with my brother and sister who didn't really seem to care about what these people were watching. I would usually, angrily, leave the room or try not to look at the TV. It also made me mad that another woman didn't care that her husband was looking at some other lady's breasts. There were also, of course, the young boys who got ahold of some dirty magazine and were passing it around their little circle of friends "Oohing" and "Aahing" at what they saw. I hated it when I would curiously take a peek and try to see what they were

looking at, only to find it to be, as expected, some naked lady whose picture was now engrained into my memory.

When my father's 3 year term in Germany was up, we were fortunate enough to be able to move back to Hawaii. Having to leave all of my friends, specifically my friend Matthias, who I had grown very close to, was hard on me because I once again had to start over and make friends all over again. I have consistently felt alone for probably the last 10 years of my life if not more. Throughout the years I have known God was always with me, but not felt like He was... I eventually made a couple of friends here and there, like my friend Jeremy whom I met in 6th grade, but I still felt alone when the day was over. Transitioning from one school to another, from being home-schooled to attending a public school, is almost as hard as moving at times because you are thrown into a whole new group of people and you are left to fend for yourself.

My life from about the age of 10 to 16 is somewhat of a blur to me. What happened when, and in what order, I do not fully recall. I have in past years done my best to

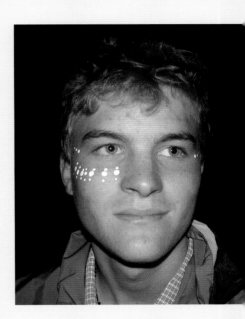

157

forget what I have done, shoving it deeper and deeper into my memory. Shortly after moving back to Hawaii, I became extremely depressed and sometimes thought about what the world would be like without me there. Would it be a better place, or worse off now that I was gone? I began to take out my pain on my family, because I did not know how to cope: arguing with them, talking back, at one point I even told my mother I hated her... something I will never forget to this day. If I could change but one thing I did in all of those years, I would take back what I said to her that sad day. I drove my father so entirely mad that he hit me for the first time in those years. I do not remember what I said, but I do know that my father, who had always disciplined us well, had to completely have lost himself to do that... something I regret having done on 3 occasions. Each of which, while I have tried to pack away in the back of my mind, to this day I cannot forget them.

During this period of my life, I began to give up on myself. My mother tells me how I used to think that I was smart, and she wonders what happened along the way. I think the biggest thing that happened to me,

started after I started fixing computers in seventh grade, and was more of a process rather than a single event. Viruses and Adware can often find their way onto the computer from ignorant users who click on some pop-up or advertisements, yes, but I would say that most things that can harm your computers host themselves in pornography. Pornography is like a virus that quickly takes hold of your mind, and yet after you give in to it, you feel so completely empty and even more alone then you did before. I began exploring the Internet, and all of the evil that it can offer, at an early age. I also, having a God given natural talent for computers, quickly learned how to cover all of my tracks, and used it for evil rather than good. To my knowledge, I have never actually been caught, sometimes wishing I would be, so that I could stop myself from what I was doing to myself. I used to open multiple Internet windows and learned how to quickly kill one of them when someone walked in, so that it looked like I was writing a paper, checking my email, playing a game, or something along those lines.

You may wonder what happened to my values and beliefs. What happened to my relationship with God, and why the sudden change of heart. Why I suddenly gave in to all of the temptations the Internet has to offer. It was not, however, a quick transition from good to bad. It was, like I previously stated, a process, a seed that started small and quickly grew. As a man, who is naturally attracted to women, while what I had seen in the past of them I found offensive in my heart and soul, I physically yearned for it. My addiction started out like a little lie that grows into a big lie. Typing in something I rationalized as being harmless, "Women" in Google search, slowly escalated into "Nude Women," etc. As I began to lose myself, and my sense of self worth, it slowly turned from single frame pictures into full-blown sex videos. Each time I gave in to the temptation, it tore off another piece of my heart. The heart that the Devil had slowly ripped to pieces. My pain was two-fold: the pain of giving in, and the pain of what have I once again just done...

I believe that my relations with women suffered, more and more, because I did not have very many physical friendships with women. Most of the women I began to see were just faces and bodies exposed for all to see on the Internet, where communication is not necessary. Not very many girls I have known have shown what I recognized to be any interest in me whatsoever. Could I blame them? Actually, the problem was me. My mind has been clouded for so long... For the last 10 years or so I have completely hated myself for what I have done to, not only myself, but to my future wife. Being someone to whom my family is so important, and to whom being the best father and husband I can possibly be, is so important too, after all I have done, how could I expect someone to love me? I didn't even love myself. In fact, like I previously stated, I at times wanted to kill myself.

My mother tells me all the time that I am her Samuel. How she prayed to have a child, after not being able to seemingly have children. How she told the Lord that she would give me back to Him, if He would just give her a child, and how I am His and not hers. That God has a special plan for my life, and that He has many blessings in store for me. The thought of hurting my parents and family and what my death would do to them, along with my fear of God, is what has kept me alive. I believe that suicide is the ultimate form of rejecting God, destroying the holy temple he built from the very dirt of this earth, destroying the life He gave to my mother as an answered prayer, the life He intends to use for His glory. If my life were so seemingly horrible and painful, how much worse would sending myself straight to hell be? I thank God for the healthy fear of Him I have been given that drives me on.

Throughout junior high and high school, I helped out with youth groups, read my bible, prayed all the time, and more importantly asked God to give me the strength to carry on. I would ask Him to help me stop doing what I was doing on the Internet. I would continually relapse into my ongoing addiction to pornography. I would be ok for a week, maybe even two, and then give up and give in, if only for a split second of pleasure, and I would then hate myself, more than ever. My heart broke for the women I was defiling with my body and mind, fueling the hatred I had inside myself more and more.

When I went to college, after graduating high school with a 3.6 GPA, I did not receive any type of scholarship or financial rewards for doing well in high school. My

drive to be excellent in school slowly faded away, as I could no longer see the point in doing my best when people who did horrible in high-school were in the same classes as me. I did well the first semester, but now that I was in college, I began questioning what I had worked so hard for. I only had a couple years, or so I thought, to figure out what I was supposed to do with my life. What was I trying to accomplish or achieve? I switched majors a couple times, and while at first I was totally pumped up and motivated to do well, my drive slowly faded away at the thought of my life being potentially meaningless. The 3rd semester in school I joined ROTC and was on track to fulfill my lifelong goal of serving in the military. I have always loved history and have wanted to serve and protect the people of this great nation. One underlying reason, however, is that I wanted to join the military to be killed in action. To die the death of an American Hero, the only way I could think of my life having any value. Having all but destroyed any love I had for myself. Those dreams were destroyed when I found out I had vocal chord dysfunction, the reason I couldn't run 5 miles without throwing up 10 times. Having to take steroids the rest of my career was not something I looked forward to doing, so I closed that door in my life.

I had completely lost sight of what was good in my life, the blessings God had given me, and dropped out of college, after starting my 4th semester and being so completely depressed and alone that I called my parents and basically told them I couldn't take it anymore. So they brought me home. Unbeknown to them, I had been doing things in my dorm room on my computer to fuel my secret addiction to one of the things I hate most in life, the objectification of women. I had stopped going to class and just slept all day or played video-games, the only things I knew would keep me from using my time for doing other things I did not want to do. My parents have always thought I played video games too much and that I was completely addicted to them. The truth is, while I do believe I have an addictive personality, I have not always so much enjoyed video games, as I have used them to take up time. Time I knew I wouldn't be studying for a test or doing homework anyway, even though I needed to.

A few months after leaving school, my dad got me a job at Hope Chapel West Oahu helping Brian Aki out with the new building project they were undertaking. Building a new facility for the church, because they were growing so fast they could not house all of the church members. I was Brian's personal helper, and I absolutely loved it. I was happy to be doing something useful with my time and efforts, happy to finally be serving God, in one form or another. Later on, I started using some of my computer skills, doing more graphic design, for the church as the building came closer to completion. They didn't need as much help with the building as they did marketing materials and graphics for sermons, and even some videos and things of that nature.

For some reason I have apparently always come across as hating kids, or at least in my younger years, but I actually love kids (unless they are screaming for no apparent reason) and am very much looking forward to having some of my own. I began helping out with the youth ministry there at Hope Chapel, something I absolutely loved. Having been blessed with wonderful parents, I saw how much these kids needed some positive influences in their lives. With the divorce rate at an all-time high, so many people nowadays are not even fortunate enough to have both of their parents living together under the same roof. We had gone to Hope Chapel before, but had left when we moved to a different part of the island. As such, when I came back, because I had gotten a job there, I knew most of the people, unless they were very new. Even then, I was able to learn most of the faces of not only the kids, but their parents too. Everyone seemed to love me, and I was always polite and courteous to everyone. Deep inside I still hated myself though, and I just could not see myself in the good light that other people did.

It was there that I met my first, and the only, girlfriend to this day thus far, whose parents would never admit that I was her boyfriend. Her name I shall not give, it is unimportant, and I do not want to hurt her any more than I potentially already have. She meant more to me than anyone could possibly know, and I grew to love her very much. I wanted to marry her with all my heart. Her parents hated me, why to this day I do not know, and caused me a great many problems, within the church

even. I was, at the same time, still severely depressed, and at times continuing to suffer from my addiction that popped up every now and then. It was not as prevalent when I had a woman to actually physically spend time with, so I spent every second I could with her.

My aunt and uncle had talked to my sister, who told them my financial situation and that I was continually depressed. I had been seeing a counselor for a long time, but was still having problems. I was not making enough working at the church to be able to support myself on my own, if I tried. They wanted to help me, and offered for me to come live with them. Eventually taking up their offer, I flew to Florida to live with them in February of 2010. Before I left, my situation with my "unofficial" girlfriend's parents just got worse and worse. They would call me just to yell at me, and later they even called me at midnight here in Florida just to lecture me further. So I eventually gave up on trying. They already hated me, why should I try to do the Godly thing and please them? So my girlfriend and I started becoming more and more passionate, although we never slept together.

162

Arriving here in February, I had to start all over from scratch: no parents, no friends, and no church. My aunt and uncle, along with my grandparents from my father's side, live here in Florida. The first couple of weeks were like a much needed vacation. After all, I had not seen any of them recently, usually only seeing them once every few years, because we always lived so far away. A few weeks later, I was back to my normal depressed self, though, and this time I really was... alone. My aunt and uncle did their best to help me have fun, and tried to get me out of the house, but I spent most of the next 4 months living in my self made hell-hole of a room. After all, the only thing I had was my computer, and I had a good Internet connection...

The first couple of months, my relationship with my girlfriend was still going strong, despite the way her parents treated us, and we talked of her coming out to visit. The downside was that we talked of doing things together that outside of the confines of marriage would have been a sin against our bodies and against God. To my benefit, not seen at the time, she abandoned me for 2 weeks and cut off all communication with me during that time. When she came back, she acted as if nothing had happened, but no longer treated me as she used to. Something had changed in her. There soon came the talk of just being friends, because "God had someone better for you Mykal" which I could not believe was happening. I did not want someone better, I wanted her. I loved her so much I did not care if there was someone better. People already had told me that I didn't want in-laws that hated me anyway, and that I was better off, but I had, up until that point, refused to listen to them. I had ignorantly also ignored the fact that she had also never said that she loved me, except on 2 occasion, where I truly believe she only said it because she felt obligated.

My life completely changed when she said those words to me. Now, not only would no woman ever love me, but also her parents would not love me either. I hated myself even more. I began to eat more and just sleep; I no longer even had the desire to play video games. They were no longer entertaining; they merely just helped me pass away the time that I felt had no meaning anyway... I started gaining weight, but no longer cared, because I hated what I saw in the mirror anyway.

In June of 2010, my uncle got me a job at Publix, where I worked in the Deli. People say it is the hardest job in the entire store, but I didn't care, I was happy to be making money. More importantly, I was happy to be doing something productive with my time, not wasting it tearing my heart out of my body, back home in my room. Working hard is something I strive to do, but there is always the question of why do I work hard, and what am I trying to achieve? My fruity nickname I was given at work is Mr. Giggles. Laughing is the single biggest thing that helps me retain my sanity in this crazy world. The single biggest thing that helps melt away some of my pain... so I try to pass it on to other people.

In October of 2010, after searching for a church I could attend, I finally visited The House: College and Young Adults Ministry at First Assembly of God in Fort Myers. I had not attended church since I had moved to Florida. I knew that I needed to do something or my life, quick, would continue to dwindle even further away from me than it already had. My current friend, Chad, was quick to befriend me, a fellow nerd who works on computers all the time, as well. Thanks Chad. Sometime around

then, I told God that I just couldn't take it anymore, that I hated myself so much for what I had been doing for years upon years, and I wanted to stop, but couldn't. I desperately needed His help. What happened exactly, I do not know, but He cut my addiction from my life. Yes, I still struggle with wanting to have an intimate relationship with a woman, but I want that woman to be my wife. I want to know that she loves me as much as I love her. To my knowledge, I have not looked at a pornographic website since last October. When I see a seductive ad on Facebook, or some other website, instead of clicking on it to see where it might magically lead me, I refresh the page until a non-threatening ad comes up.

I still suffer greatly with my self-confidence and lust. I pray to the Lord everyday to give me strength and wisdom, to make me the man of God He wants me to be. To become the man my future wife and kids need me to be. Looking in the mirror, and slowly realizing that I don't have to hate what I see anymore, is a new concept. Realizing that God has been here, beside me the entire time, carrying me in my darkest hours, as it says in the poem "Footprints in the Sand." Knowing that God loves and adores me more than I could ever know, and that He forgave me, before I ever committed my vast and many sins. That there is a woman out there, who will forgive me for what I have done, and love me no less. Who will be the only one I dream of at night, when I lay there beside her, watching her as she sleeps, praying, thanking God for giving me a gift that I didn't deserve.

Learning to love something you hate is difficult in itself, but drawing closer to God than ever before, is harder. It takes strong discipline, and the active seeking of Him. I told God I would spend time with Him every day, whether it be watching a sermon and/or reading my bible, no matter how I horrible or tired I feel. I also journal 5 things that I am thankful for, before I go to sleep each night. So that, when I go to bed each night, I do so being thankful for what God has done in my life, rather than going to bed angry and depressed, as I used to do each night. Thinking to myself, "Hey I look pretty good today" rather than thinking that I am ugly, and that no women are attracted to me. Knowing that God is right here beside me, always, even when I forget to thank or ask Him to be. He will never leave me, or forsake me, ever. No matter how much I don't feel like He is there... He always will be.

I am a work in progress, having to take things one step at a time. As my mother would say, I am "A Cracked Egg" and God is slowly putting me back together. He is also showing me that I am unique and special to Him. While all eggs are eggs, not one is exactly like another, no matter how similar they may look. Step by step, I am moving forward and learning not to look back at the things I have done. The things that I can no longer change. I must be bold and courageous, striving to be a man after God's own heart like the Lord's servant David. To be weird for Him as Craig Groeschel pastor of Lifechurch.tv would say, and to not worry about my future, because He holds me in the palm of His hands, and always watches over me, and will direct my steps.

Old Rod vs. a New One

In these times of
technological advances, the
average fly fisherman follo[ws]
the trend, but slowly. Tak[e]
that fiberglass rod that I[...]
had for years. It still ca[sts]
as well as it ever did. I[n]
fact, it seems like it ca[sts]
better. It's better mayb[e]
because my skills using [...]
have improved. Don't for[get]
cleaned up those snakes [and]
the ceramic eyes.

The line feels improve[d]
is the same one we di[d]
too much last year. I[...]
that new line dressin[g]
opened a fresh bottl[e of]
floatant. I remember[...]
renew the line's kn[ow]
sure they all are c[...]
tight, and smooth. [...]
I even remembered t[o]
the reel to [...]
with the [...]

1

Fishing for [...]

really popu[lar]

water for qu[...]

bass so we a[...]

pan size. Tha[t]

THE END

I would like to express a huge Hawaiian "Mahalo", or thank you, for joining me on this wild journey. The Tackle Box has made a huge impact in my life in a very short period of time and I believe it can make a tremendous difference in your life, too. My heart's desire is that you have been challenged enough to continue on to the workbook and to TackleBoxBook.com for additional resources, pictures, testimonials, and engaging stories. My prayer is that you have learned more about yourself, more about the Fisherman, and how to recognize the lures that he casts before you. I also hope that you can use the strategies I have set forth to avoid those lures. And, if you are already hooked, I pray that you can successfully and victoriously disentangle yourself. I look forward to hearing from you and I am truly excited to see how we can all dive deeper together...

10

V.L.Daubenspeck WS_T
Fishing the Flats
Word count 946

FISHING THE FLATS

e lunkers in Southern Arizona's arid back country is not

My family and I have been going to this one piece of

a few years. We have caught more than our share of

big advocates of the catch and release all but a few fry-

ay be why we like it so much.

TACKLE BOX: MORE THANKS

After my Dad passed in August of 2013, there were really only a few things he left behind that I absolutely had to have. I wanted a couple of Aikido and fishing books and I unquestionably had to have the fishing lures that we used across the lakes of Arizona. I packed them up and brought them 4600 miles back to my home here in Hawaii. As the book unfolded, I knew I wanted to have the lures professionally photographed and I have to express my deep gratitude to Dave Sanford for making it happen.

Dave took an immediate interest in making sure that he captured the essence of what I was looking for and his attention to detail was amazing. The pictures he took immortalize the memories I have on the water with my father and I will forever be grateful. The lures you see in this book are from that collection. Thank you Dave from the bottom of my heart. (DaveSanfordStudios.com)

I believe it was a divine appointment when I walked into the Hana Pa'a Fishing and Dive Company in Kalihi. While waiting for my wife's first post-graduate interview to finish, I decided to kill some time looking at all the flashy freediving equipment, but what really caught my eye was a new book near the cash register. *The Evolution of Freediving* was beautiful and everything I imagined the book I was formulating in my head would look like. After talking with Sterling Kaya behind the counter, he arranged a meeting with his team at FLUID Media Publishing, and the quest soon began. I would like to thank Sterling for indulging me as I walked around the store apprehensively relaying my vision. I would also like to thank Clifford Cheng of VOICE Design for his unparalleled design creativity and patience in dealing with me and the direction I saw this project heading. I could not have asked for a better team to put my dreams in print. I also thank you guys from the bottom of my heart. (hanapaafishing.com) (fluidmediahawaii.com)

Thank you Chris Wall for your friendship and professional design and creation of the book's website (TackleBoxBook.com). Your belief in the project translated into a great visual experience and I look forward to our collaboration as this passionate endeavor continues to grow. Thank you, thank you, thank you. (Lolopages.com)

Finally, thank you to everyone that submitted photos for publication. It was so much fun to see the photos and reflect on all of the memories around them. I can't wait for more adventures and I look forward to seeing pictures of your travels along with your trophy fish.

Please visit: TackleBoxBook.com